OUTRAGEOUS JAPANESE

SLANG, CURSES & EPITHETS

Revised Edition

by Jack Seward

D0681425

TUTTLE PUBLISHING
Tokyo • Rutland, Vermont • Singapore

Published by Tuttle Publishing, an imprint of Periplus Editions (HK) Ltd., with editorial offices at 61 Tai Seng Avenue, #02-12, Singapore 534167 and 364 Innovation Drive, North Clarendon, Vermont 05759 U.S.A.

LCC card No. 91-65059
ISBN 13: 978-4-8053-0848-6
ISBN 10: 4-8053-0848-6

Distributed by

North America, Latin America & Europe
Tuttle Publishing
364 Innovation Drive,
North Clarendon, VT 05759-9436 U.S.A.
Tel: 1 (802) 773-8930
Fax: 1 (802) 773-6993
info@tuttlepublishing.com
www.tuttlepublishing.com

Japan
Tuttle Publishing
Yaekari Building, 3rd Floor,
5-4-12 Osaki, Shinagawa-ku
Tokyo 141-0032
Tel: (81) 3 5437-0171
Fax: (81) 3 5437-0755
tuttle-sales@gol.com

Asia Pacific
Berkeley Books Pte. Ltd.
61 Tai Seng Avenue, #02-12
Singapore 534167
Tel: (65) 6280-1330
Fax: (65) 6280-6290
inquiries@periplus.com.sg
www.periplus.com

11 10 09 08 07   6 5 4 3

Printed in Singapore

For

Corky and Mary Alexander

Contents

Introduction

It is often taken as an article of faith that the amiable, soft-spoken Japanese seldom resort to verbal abuse or defamation in their dealings with others. All the same, while I was attending Japanese language school, our top-priority mission was acquiring the vocabulary needed to (a) roundly malign others, and (b) become cozy with Oriental maidens when we at last reached the distant, misty shores of Japan. The harvest of the second task was indeed much more bountiful than the first.

But I persevered and at length came to understand that the Japanese language — if not a cornucopia of curses and censure — is at least rich enough to reasonably satisfy occasional compulsions to condemn and recriminate. Granted, the Japanese strive for surface harmony and try to avoid antagonistic confrontations when possible. As a result, quantitatively speaking, they do not generate verbal vitriol in the quantity or variety that can be attributed to some other nationalities. But this is not to suggest that they are without their resources. As you will see herein, they can be inventive users of invective that is both vivid and injurious.

Before you begin this adventure in aspersion, let me refresh your memory about what really effective malediction sounds like in English.

The *Harper's Weekly* once reviled president Abraham Lincoln in these words:

   "Filthy storyteller, despot, liar, thief, braggart, buffoon, usurper, monster, Ignoramus Abe, Old

Scoundrel, perjurer, robber, swindler, tyrant, field-butcher, land-pirate."

Reading such a diatribe, the reader might be tempted to feel sorry for poor old Abe, saddled as he was with Marfan's syndrome and a vicious harpy of a wife. Surely there are politicians teeming underfoot today who are more richly deserving of such disparagement than Lincoln was.

Or consider what Martin Luther wrote about Henry VIII of England:

"... a pig, an ass, a dunghill, the spawn of an adder, a basilisk, a lying buffoon, a mad fool with a frothy mouth, a lubberly ass ... a frantic madman."

In more recent times (1953), East German Communists serving as spokesmen of their government aspersed Englishmen in general in these pejorative terms:

"Paralytic sycophants, effete betrayers of humanity, carrion-eating servile imitators, arch-cowards and collaborators, gang of women murderers, degenerate rabble, parasitic traditionalists, playboy soldiers, conceited dandies."

Although not really in the same class, the Japanese have been known to besmirch others with broadsides that should at least get the attention of the party denigrated. Author Yukio Mishima once anathematized Japanese intellectuals with this bit of vituperation:

"... their cowardice, sneering 'objectivity,' rootlessness, dishonesty, flunkeyism, mock gestures of resistance, self-importance, inactivity, talkativeness, and readiness to eat their own words."
(Quoted in *The Life and Death of Yukio Mishima*, by Henry Scott Stokes)

However they stack up against their foreign competitors, the Japanese certainly have sufficient weapons in their armory to offend and discredit those they feel need lambasting.

Guide to Pronunciation

Japanese vowels are always pronounced the same:

a	like the **a** in f**a**ther
e	like the **e** in **e**gg
i	like the **e** in m**e**
o	like the **o** in **o**h
u	like the first **u** in **Z**u**lu

You will find macrons (lines) over some vowels. Differentiating between "long" and "short" vowels is important. Saying **kuso** 糞 instead of **kusō** 苦僧 or **komon** 顧問 instead of **kōmon** 肛門 will evince laughter, incomprehension, or embarrassment.

There are only two other sounds that may require some effort to master:

tsu	Place the tip of your tongue behind your upper front teeth and say the girl's name "Sue."
r	This is a lightly tapped **r** which lies between the English **r** and **d**.

Although there is a slight pitch in Japanese, you should utter all your Japanese words and sentences in an even tone like the tick-tock-tick-tock of a metronome. The final **u** う in the **–masu** ます form of verbs and **desu** です is usually silent.

CHAPTER ONE
Physical Appearance

FAT OR SKINNY

The Japanese language is rich in words to hurt others through disparaging comments about weight, shape, age, attire, odor, and hairiness. Let's look first at several choice words of abuse that can be directed at those who are, bluntly speaking, **futotte iru** 太っている (fat). There is a very good (and obvious) reason that I know a god's plenty of such colorful epithets, enough of them having been directed at my person.

I must note, however, that the Japanese may not all agree that such words are belittling. Although the younger generation wants to be "smart" (meaning fashionably slender, not intelligent), the older ones tend to regard obesity as obvious proof of success and wealth. Else, how could you afford to eat enough to put on that extra weight? Indeed, the word for paunch is **jūyaku-bara** 重役腹, or "a company director's stomach."

I shudder to recall how often a Japanese acquaintance (I disdain to use the word friend) has launched at me a brutal barb like:

> **Mā, Suwādo-san wa honto ni futotte iru, ne.**
> まあ、スワードさんは本当に太っているね。
> You really are fat, aren't you, Mr. Seward.

I try to keep in mind that my acquaintance may have meant his comment as a compliment of sorts but it has taken me a long time to accustom myself to such a frank evaluation, a very long time indeed.

Other words which can be used to describe excessive weight include **debu-debu** でぶでぶ and **buyo-buyo** ぶよぶよ, as in these examples:

> **Buchō no debu-debu shita musume wa yobanaide okō. Kanojo no shiri ni au isu wa nai kara na.**
> 部長のでぶでぶした娘は呼ばないでおこう。彼女の尻に合う椅子はないからな。
> Let's not invite the section chief's obese daughter. We don't have a chair that would fit her hips.

> **O-debu no musume** おでぶの娘 fatty girl

> **Ano buyo-buyo bāsan wa anata ni te wo futte iru.**
> あのぶよぶよ婆さんは、あなたに手を振っている。
> That flabby old woman is waving her hand at you.

That same **buyo-buyo bāsan** ぶよぶよ婆さん would be expected to have pendulous breasts, the word for which is **tare-jichi** 垂れ乳 "hanging breasts". Thus, if the circumstances indicate, she could also be called:

- **tare-jichi no hihi-babā** 垂れ乳の狒狒婆
  baboonlike old woman with saggy breasts

A flat-chested woman can be described as **pecha-pai** ぺちゃぱい, the **pecha** ぺちゃ coming from **pechanko ni naru** ぺちゃんこになる, "to be flattened":

> **Kare wa pecha-pai to kekkon shita.**
> 彼はぺちゃぱいと結婚した。
> He married a girl who has no tits at all.

Other germane expressions:

- **deppuri shita (hito)** でっぷりした（人）dumpy (person)
- **toshima-butori** 年増太り a gain in weight that women may experience with the encroachment of middle age
- **zunguri shita (hito)** ずんぐりした（人）fat and short (person)
- **hyakkan debu** 百貫でぶ tub of lard (**hyakkan** 百貫 means 100 **kan** 貫 or 826 pounds.)
- **futotcho** 太っちょ blimp

In contrast to such heavyweights, we have the skinny ones. **Yaseru** 痩せる is the verb meaning to lose weight, and from it derives **yase-koketa** 痩せこけた "to be emaciated".

Sono yase-koketa otoko wa byōki ni chigai nai.
その痩せこけた男は病気に違いない。
That emaciated man has to be sick.

Hisashiburi ni Abe-san ni atta ga miru kage mo naku yasete ita. 久しぶりに安部さんに会ったが、見る影もなく痩せていた。
I met Mr. Abe for the first time in a long while. He was a mere shadow of his former self (lit., so thin as not to even have a shadow).

Sō da yo. Hone to kawa bakari sa.
そうだよ。骨と皮ばかりさ。That's right. He's just skin and bones (lit., bones and hide).

Wags who wish to personalize this description can construct such name as:

- **Honekawa Sujiko** 骨皮筋子 Miss Sujiko Honekawa (lit., Miss Sinewy Bonehide)

This reminds me of how a friend once depicted such a woman. He said, "Putting your arms around her is like putting your arms around a sack of antlers."

Such ridicule can be extended to men by using this name:

- **Honekawa Sujio** 骨皮筋雄 Mr Sinewy Bonehide
  (The final **o** お indicates it is a male name, where-as a final **ko** こ signals a feminine name.)

There is a class of Buddhist ascetics who fast for religious purposes. Like Mahatma Ghandhi, these holy men usually do not have enough excess fat on them to feed a gnat for a day. They are called:

- **rakan** 羅漢 skin-and-bones Buddhist fanatics
  (The word was once applied to Buddha's five hun-dred disciples who had entered into the state of Nirvana.)

In the last extreme, those fleshless ones become mere:

- **ikeru shikabane** 生ける屍 living corpses

Men who are not necessarily fat but whose bone structure (**hone-gumi** 骨組み) is huge can be disparaged with words like these:

- **udo** うど great awkward oaf

Ō-otoko sōmi ni chie ga mawari-kane
大男総身に知恵が回りかね The brain power of a big man does not extend throughout his body.

That is how the proverb translates but it's easier just to say, "You dumb lout."

A David next to such a Goliath could be cut down with the following:

- **chinchikurin** ちんちくりん dwarfish
- **kobito** 小人 pygmy, runt, shrimp
- **issun-bōshi** 一寸法師 Tom Thumb (lit., a one-inch monk)

Nani? Ore wa issun-bōshi datte? Kisama wa keshikaran kobito ja nai ka. なに。俺は一寸法師だって。貴様は怪しからん小人じゃないか。
What? I'm a Tom Thumb? Why, you're nothing but an insolent runt, aren't you!

FACE
- **nikibi-zura** にきび面 pimple-covered face
- **chimmurui no kao** 珍無類の顔 face that would stop a clock
- **umeboshi-gao** 梅干顔 prune face
- **minikui kao** 醜い顔 ugly face

Yukiko no minikui kao wo mita dake de mushizu ga hashiru. 由紀子の醜い顔を見ただけで虫唾が走る。
The mere sight of Yukiko's ugly face sends chills down my back.

Iinazuke no kao wo mita dake de Tomoe wa muna-kuso ga waruku natta.
許婚の顔を見ただけで友恵は胸糞が悪くなった。
The mere sight of her fiance's face nauseated Tomoe.

- **sukebē** 助平 lecherous face

Tarehoho no sukebē na tsuragamae datta.
垂れ頬の助平な面構えだった。
It was a lecherous face with drooping jowls.

Sayuri wa me mo aterarenai kurai hidoi kao desu.
小百合は目も当てられないくらい酷い顔です。
Sayuri's face is too awful to look at.

The following three words are all used to mean a stupid-looking face:

- **baka-zura** 馬鹿づら
- **ahō-zura** 阿呆づら
- **manuke-zura** 間抜けづら

EYES
- **yani-me** やに目 rheumy-eyed
- **hingara-me** ひんがら目 cross-eyed (**Suga-me** すが目 means the same as **hingara-me** ひんがら目)
- **de-me** 出目 popeyed lecher
- **donguri-manako** どんぐり眼 goggle-eyed (**donguri** どんぐり is acorn; **manako** 眼 is another word for eyes).
- **kirenaga no me** 切れ長の目 slit-eyes
- **tsuri-me** つり目 slant-eyed
- **Ron-Pari** ロンパリ wall-eyes (lit., London-Paris eyes)

Imagin that you are standing athwart the English Channel and are looking at both the cities simultaneously.

MOUTH
- **wani-guchi** 鰐口 mouth of a crocodile
- **ha-nuke** 歯抜け toothless
- **deppa** 出っ歯 buck-toothed (**Soppa** 反っ歯 also means buck-toothed or, according to some sources, snaggle-toothed.)

Iki no kusaki wa nushi shirazu.
息の臭きは主知らず
One is not aware of his own foul breath.

This is a literary expression used to describe someone who is blissfully unaware of his own faults. This is not, however, the case for the unfortunates around him.

NOSE
- **kagi-bana** 鈎鼻 hook-nosed
- **tongari-bana** とんがり鼻 pointed nose
- **hanatare kozō** 洟垂れ小僧 snot-nosed brat

VOICE
- **shagare-goe** 嗄れ声 hoarse-voiced

FOREHEAD
- **dekosuke** デコ助 beetle-browed

HAIR
- **kebukai** 毛深い hairy
- **hage-atama** 禿げ頭 bald
- **ketō** 毛唐 hairy barbarian (usually meaning a Westerner)

Kanojo no oppai ni wa kowakute kuroi ke ga haete iru-tte.
彼女のおっぱいには強くて黒い毛が生えているって。
I hear she has coarse black hairs growing out of her tits.

- **kedarake** 毛だらけ hairy
- **paipan** パイパン woman with no crotch hair

LEGS
- **soto-ashi** 外足 knock-knees
- **ganimata** がに股 bow-legged

ODOR
- **tsube-kuso-kusai** つべ糞臭い smelling of **tsube-kuso** つべ糞 (The word **tsube-kuso** つべ糞 covers

a lot of ground. I have heard it used to refer to smegma, crotch cheese, toe jam, and dingle-berries.)

ATTIRE
- **buzama na minari** 無様な身なり unsightly appearance
- **musakurushi minari** むさ苦しい身なり shabby attire

RAVAGES OF AGE
- **boke-babā/jijī** ボケ婆/爺 senile old strumpet
- **oni-babā** 鬼婆 devilish old harpy, hell-hag
- **ha-nuke-babā/jijī** 歯抜け婆/爺 toothless old bat
- **samehada-babā** 鮫肌婆 old woman with coarse-grained skin (lit., shark skin)
- **shiwakucha-babā/jijī** 皺くちゃ婆/爺 wrinkled old crone
- **oibore-babā/jijī** 老いぼれ婆/爺 gross and aging hag
- **kusottare-babā/jijī** 糞ったれ婆/爺 shitty old goat

Note: Substitute **jijī** for **babā** when referring to old men.

JUST PLAIN UGLY
- **subeta** スベタ relentlessly ugly woman, gorgon
- **futame to mirarenai** 二目と見られない shock-ing, hideous (lit., can't look at twice)
- **busu** ブス homely slattern
- **okachimenko** おかちめんこ unsightly wench
- **akujo** 悪女 repulsive female
- **bu-otoko** ブ男 ugly brute
- **hyottoko** ひょっとこ ugly person, gargolye, dis-torted face mask

Anna hyottoko to kokkon suru nante tondemo-nai ze.

あんなひょっとこと結婚するなんてとんでもないぜ。

The thought of marrying such an ugly person is simply out of the question.

MISCELLANEOUS

Japanese children have a chant that goes: **Omaeno kāsan debeso!** おまえのかあさんでべそ！ Literally it means, "Your mother has a protruding navel!" It is akin to, "Your mother wears flour-sack drawers (or surplus army boots)." It is not meant as a compliment.

This chant was popularized in 1965 by a comic group called Hana Hajime and the Crazy Cats ハナ肇とクレイジーキャッツ. The full, somewhat incomprehensible chant ran:

Baka. Kaba. Chindon-ya. バカ カバ チンドン屋
Fool. Hippo. Street musician.

Omae no kāchan debeso. お前のかあちゃんでべそ
Your mom's belly button sticks out.

Omae no tōchan nana-iro debeso.
お前のとうちゃん七色でべそ
Your dad's belly button has seven colors.

Mimi no ana kara te tsukkonde okuba gata-gata iwasetaru de.
耳の穴から手突っ込んで奥歯ガタガタ言わせたるで
I'll stick a hand in your ear and rattle around your back teeth.

Mendō mikirenē nā. 面倒見切れね～な～
I just can't look after you.

CHAPTER TWO
Threats, Taunts and Curses

Here is a prime selection of threats, curses, zingers, and rough commands as well as an ample supply of caustic words of chastisement, cautions, and sharp retorts.

I have given figurative translations (unless otherwise noted) since literal ones often fail to get the offensive ideas across. For instance: **sono te wa kuwan zo.** その手は食わんぞ. Literally this translates as, "I won't eat that hand." Since that doesn't really say much, I have elected to give readers a more figurative rendering. In this instance:

Sono te wa kuwan zo.　その手は食わんぞ。
None of your bloody tricks now.

THREATS
Needless to say, there are hundreds, even thousands of phrases and sentences that are used to intimidate others. But since a complete list is out of the question. I have chosen a few as a starter kit:

Myō na ki wo okosu na.　妙な気を起こすな。
Don't try anything funny.

Sunao ni naran to buchi-nomesu ze.
素直にならんとぶちのめすぜ。　If you don't do what I say, I'm going to beat the hell out of you.

Shikaeshi suru zo.　仕返しするぞ。
I'll get even (for that).

Itai me ni awaseru zo!　痛い目にあわせるぞ！
You're going to feel it from me!

Hitotsu yaki wo irete yaru beki da.
つ焼きを入れてやるべきだ。
I should teach you a lesson.

Mogaite mo shiyō ga nai.　もがいても仕様がない。
It's no use struggling.

Aitsu yattsukete yaru.　あいつ、やっつけてやる。
I'll fix him.

Omote e dero.　表へ出ろ。Step outside.

Keri wo tsukeyō.　ケリをつけよう。
Let's settle this or Let's put an end to this.

The expression **keri wo tsukeru** ケリをつける comes from
Japanese **tanka** 短歌 and **haiku** 俳句 poems, which often
end with the auxiliary verb **keri** ケリ. Thus, "to add a **keri**
ケリ" means to bring things to an end.

Beso wo kakuzo.　べそをかくぞ。
You'll be sorry for this.

Beso wo kaku べそをかく
literally means to be on the verge of tears, to snivel
and whimper.

Ato de totchimete yaru.　あとでとっちめてやる。
I'll make you smart later.

Doteppara ni kaza-ana wo akete yaru kara oboete oke. どてっ腹に風穴を開けてやるから覚えておけ。
Remember, I'm going to drill a hole in your dirty guts.

This old expression was something used by swordsmen in the **chambara** movies, but it could also be said by a modern-day gangster pointing a pistol at a foe's stomach.

Seibai shite kureru. 成敗してくれる。
I'll destroy you.

Omae wo hakusei ni shiteyaru.
お前を剥製にしてやる。
I'll have you stuffed and mounted.

TAUNTS

In Japanese the choice of pronoun for the speaker or the person spoken to can determine the degree of politeness or rudeness. **Ore** 俺, for instance, is a haughty word for "I." Its use often suggests that you feel superior to the person you are addressing.

The man who uses **ore** is likely to use **omae** お前 or **kisama** 貴様 to mean "you." **Kisama** 貴様 is a notch below **omae** お前 in rudeness, so if you resent being addressed as **omae** お前, you should try this as a fiery retort:

Omae to wa nan da, kisama! お前とは何だ、貴様！
What the devil do you (**kisama** 貴様) mean by having the audacity to address me as **omae** お前?

Kisama doko no dobu kara waitan da?
貴様どこのドブから湧いたんだ。
What sewer did you crawl out of?

Or if the other fellow persists in his rudeness, one could try:

Dare ni mono wo ii-agatterun da?
誰にものを言あがってるんだ。
Just who the hell do you think you're talking to?

Ii-agaru 言いあがる means to speak up to someone. Its use makes it crystal-clear that you consider the person to whom you are talking to be far beneath you.

Continuing the assault, one might say:

Namaiki ja nai ka. 生意気じゃないか。
You're damned impudent.

After that, this barb is flung at the wretch:

Omae no taido wa nattoran.
お前の態度はなっとらん。
Your attitude is really insufferable.

Finally, now that he's on his knees, he's finished off with:

Kisama no babā wo yatchaō.
貴様の婆をヤッちゃおう。 Screw your mother.

And lastly, I want to note a toast popular during World War II. For years I have treasured this little gem without knowing just where I might ever make use of it. Once or twice I was tempted to rise to my unsteady feet in a Roppongi pub and shout it above the din of the revelers. I didn't, but if I had, I wonder if those making merry carouse would have cheered, thrown me out, or merely ignored me.

Probably they would have muttered **hen na gaijin** 変な外人 (strange foreigner) in their **sakazuki** 杯 (saké cups) and looked away in embarrassment. Anyway, here it is:

Shinshū fumetsu, kichiku Bei-Ei!
神州不滅、鬼畜米英！ The Divine Land will never die; down with the American and British fiends!

FAMILIAL BLISS

In Japan, it is said that the family that bathes together stays together ... with minimal discord. But now Japan must gird its loincloth (**fundoshi wo shimeru** 褌を締める) and face up to the harsh realities of **kokusai-ka** 国際化 (internation-alization). The day may soon come when the Japanese will have to endure their own adaptations of American-style soap operas and sit-coms:

* *

scene: Eight-mat sitting room in a modest home in Adachi-ku 足立区, Tokyo 東京.
time: After the evening meal
onstage: A weary father, harried mother, and lustful daughter poised to go boy-hunting

* *

Daughter:　**Otōsan, kuruma no kagi wā.**
　　　　　お父さん、車の鍵はー。
　　　　　Father, where are the car keys?

Father :　**Aruite-ke yo.** 歩いてけよ。You can walk.

Daughter :　**Zakenna yo.** ざけんなよ。Cut the bull.

Father :　**Nani. Kono kono komusume me!**
　　　　　Kuruma wo kashitara mata jikoru daro.
　　　　　なに。この小娘め！車を貸したらまた事故るだろ。
　　　　　What? You cheeky wench! If I lend you
　　　　　the car, you'll just have another wreck.

Daughter : **Jikoru? Nani sore.**　事故る？　何それ。
Wreck? What is it?

Father : **Tobokeru na.**　とぼけるな。
Don't play dumb with me.

Daughter (aside to audience): **Kono boke-jijī.**
このぼけジジイ。 Old fool.

Enter Mother with next-door neighbor. Father has
lurched to his feet and is looking around wild-eyed
for a heavy, blunt object.

Father (shouting): **Kono zūzūshī surekkarashi ni
namerarete tamaru ka!**　この図々しいす
れっからしに舐められてたまるか！
I can't stand being made a fool of by this
brazen hussy.

Mother: **Hito-sama no temae mo arun dakara,
mō yoshinasai.**　人様の手前もあるんだか
ら、もうよしなさい。
Don't you see we have company? Can't
you cut it out?

Daughter (to mother): **Yokei na kuchi dashi sunna
yo, kono kuso babā.**
余計な口出しすんなよ。このクソババア。
Butt out, you old shitt.

Father (livid with anger): **Nan dato. Kuchi no kiki-
kata ni ki wo tsukero!**
なんだと。口の利き方に気をつけろ。
Wha-at? Watch your mouth.

Daughter (flouncing out in a huff): **Kuso jijī,
kutabare!**　クソジジイ、くたばれ！
You can drop dead, you old fool!

EPITHETS

When one sees or hears someone involved in difficulties he deserves and has likely brought on himself, the warmth felt deep inside oneself can be expressed with the following expressions:

Zama miro. ざま見ろ It serves (him) right.

Zama miyāgare. ざま見やがれ。
(This has the same meaning as the above expression but is even harsher in tone.)

Ii kimi da. いい気味だ。 (same as the above two)
Note that this **kimi** 気味 is not the pronoun "you" but rather two separate characters meaning "sensation" or "feeling." Thus, "It gives me a good feeling to see him in that fix."

Nameru na. 舐めるな。Sez you
(lit., Don't hold me lightly).

Dekē kao wo suru na. でけえ顔をするな。
Don't act uppity with me (lit., Don't make a big face). **Dekē** でけえ is rough for **dekai** でかい.

Kuso! 糞！Shit!

Kao wo arattte koi. 顔を洗って来い。
Wipe your nose (lit., Go wash your face.)

Shomben de kao wo aratte koi.
ションベンで顔を洗って来い。
(like the above but worse) Literally it means "Go wash your face with piss."

Te-yande. てやんで。
What the devil are you talking about?

Nani itte yande. 何言ってやんで。 (ditto)

Namakoku na ナマこくな。 Don't sass me.

Urusē. うるせえ。 Don't bug me! (Street patois for
Urusai! うるさい)

Ussē. うっせえ。 (same as above)

Yogoreru 汚れる is a verb meaning "to become
dirty." Its stem **yogore** 汚れ means "filth" or "dirt."
Thus: **Kono yogore!** この汚れ！ You scumbag!

In the same vein:

Kono o-kama. このオカマ。 You fag.

Kono hajisarashi-me. この恥さらしめ。
You're a disgrace.

Kono baita-me. この売女め。 You whore.

Abusing taxi drivers has long been a pastime in Japan, at
least among foreign residents. I had my share of run-ins
with this class, usually because they were surly, impolite,
and reckless. At length, I had two cards printed in large
quantities and always carried a supply with me, together
with a small roll of Scotch tape.

Whenever I decided that the driver needed heated chastisement, I would tape one or the other of these cards on the
back of the front seat, where all subsequent passengers
could see it. (Both are quoted from *Japanese in Action* by
the same author.)

One card read:

**Jōkyaku no mina-sama: Saikin untenshu-bushoku
ni tsuki Nihongo mo roku-ni hanasenai mugaku
no kumosuke wo yatowazaru wo emasen. Igo
taido wo aratamesase-masu node, go-ryōshō kuda-
saimase. Untenshu Torishimari-kyoku** 乗客の皆
様：最近運転手不足につき日本語もロクに話せない無
学の雲助を雇わざるをえません。以後態度を改めさせ
ますので、ご了承くださいませ。運転手取締り局
To all passengers: Recently, because of the driver
shortage, taxi companies have been forced to hire
uneducated **kumosuke** 雲助 who cannot even speak
our national language correctly. Henceforth, we will
see to it that they damned well change their attitude,
so please bear with us this time. (Signed) Driver
Control Bureau

The other card read:

**Jōkyaku no mina-sama: saikin takushī-busoku ni
tsuki arappoi unten wo sezaru wo emasen node,
seimei hoken ni haitte kara go-jōsha kudasai
masu yō o-negai mōshiage masu. Unten-shu**
乗客の皆様：最近タクシー不足につき、荒っぽい運転
をせざるを得ませんので、生命保険に入ってからご乗
車くださいますようお願い申し上げます。運転手
To all passengers: Because of the present taxi shortage, we cannot avoid driving recklessly. Please be
sure that your life insurance is up-to-date before you
board this taxi. (Signed) Your driver

Your attention is invited to the word **kumosuke** 雲助, the
Chinese characters for which literally mean "cloud fellow."
This term had its origins in the Edo period when it referred
to palanquin bearers who transported people and luggage.

These men often had no set abode and, like clouds, moved about looking for customers. Today it refers to a low-class driver of the kind described above: surly, rude, and guilty of **arappoi unten** 荒っぽい運転 (reckless driving).

When bandying libelous verbal abuse with such drivers, a potent barb would be:

> **Nani? Kumosuke no kuse ni.** なに？雲助のくせに。
> What the? ... Why, you're nothing but a low-class driver.

ROUGH COMMANDS
When irritated with someone who persists in getting in the way, one can say:

> **Doita, doita!** どいた、どいた！ Get out of the way!

The English translation is mild in tone, but in Japanese it's rough indeed. Even stronger is **Dokyāgare!** どきゃあがれ！ or **Yokero!** よけろ！

In samurai times, feudal retainers would precede their **daimyō** 大名 shouting to peasants on the road:

> **Shita ni! Shita ni!** 下に！下に！
> Bow down, bow down!

All Japanese have seen enough **chambara** ちゃんばら movies to know the expression. This is not to be used unless you really want to rouse the ire of people in your path.

Modern ways of telling anyone to disappear include:

> **Sassato usero.** さっさと失せろ。 Get lost.

Doko ka itchae. どこか行っちゃえ。
Get out of my sight.

Soko noke. そこのけ。 Move aside.

This is also a very rough expression, not something you should use with your mother-in-law, no matter how sorely tempted.

Totto to kaere! とっとと帰れ！ Get out!

Use the following as circumstances dictate:

Shikujiru na. しくじるな。Don't screw it up.

Katte na netsu wo fukun ja nai.
勝手な熱を吹くんじゃない。
None of your damned impudence.

Tsubekobe iu na, kono zubekō.
つべこべ言うな。このズベ公。
Enough of your complaints, you wench.

Yokē na o-sewa da. 余計なお世話だ。
None of your blasted business.

Ōki na o-sewa da. 大きなお世話だ。
None of your bloody business.

Jibun no atama no hae wo oe.
自分の頭の蠅を追え。Mind your damned business
(lit., Chase the flies off your own head).

Ore ni oyabun-kaze wo fukasete mo hajimaran zo.
俺に親分風を吹かせても始まらんぞ。
Don't play the big shot with me.

Mono-ii ni ki wo tsukero. 物言いに気をつけろ。
Watch your tongue.

Now we lower our standards a little:

He de mo kurae. 屁でも食らえ。
You just try it (lit., Eat my fart).

Kuso kurae. 糞食らえ。Eat shit.

If you hear such phrases, you can say:

Gesu-na koto wo iu na. ゲスなことを言うな。
Don't talk dirty.

CURSES
We begin with definitions:

- **norou** 呪う to curse
- **nonoshiru** 罵る to verbally abuse
- **akutai wo tsuku** 悪態をつく to use abusive language
- **akkō suru** 悪口する to revile
- **noroi wo kakeru** 呪いをかける to place a curse on

Three fundamental curses all meaning basically the same are:

Chikushō! 畜生！Damn (you)! or Curses (on you)!

Kuso! 糞！**Ima-imashii!** 忌々しい！

These words can be used in a general sense (Damn it all) or specifically (Damn you). They are puzzling inasmuch as the basic meaning of each differs. As we will see in the chapter on animal-related insults, **Chikushō** 畜生 actually means "beast" while **kuso** 糞 is "shit" and **ima-imashii** 忌々しい is an adjective meaning "vexing" or "irritating." Nonetheless, all are used to convey the same thing.

"Drop dead" is translated directly into Japanese as **Shinde shimae** 死んでしまえ (lit., Die and be done with it). You can also say **Shinyāgare** 死にゃあがれ, which could be given as "Die in the presence of a superior," namely, the speaker.

> **Kutabare!** くたばれ! Drop dead! or Curse you!

> **Kutabatte shimae! (Kutabatchimae)**
> くたばってしまえ。（くたばっちまえ）Drop dead!

A rather strange curse:

> **Kuso shite shine!** 糞して死ね！Shit and then die!

> **Kuso shite nero!** 糞して寝ろ！Shit and go to sleep
> (I confess that I see little connection between death, defecation, and deep slumber.)

Other potent curses are:

> **Bachi de mo ataryāgare.** 罰でも当たりゃあがれ。
> The devil take you (him/her) *or* Go to hell.

Bachi 罰 or **batsu** 罰 is "punishment from God," and **ataru** 当たる is "to befall or strike." Thus, "May punishment strike you."

> **Kono bachi-atari-me!** この罰当たりめ！

Although this has the same meaning as the preceding expression, you could never figure it out from the grammar. The sentence literally translates as "this punishment-befall-en fellow."

Other such expressions:

Katte ni shiro! 勝手にしろ！
Do whatever you please and be damned!

Berammē! べらんめえ！
Damn you, you bloody fool!

The following expression is used in utter exasperation with someone who is being simply too ridiculous for words:

Tōfu no kado ni atama wo butsukete shinjimae.
豆腐の角に頭をぶつけて死んじまえ。 Drop dead!
(lit., Hit your head on a corner of tofu and die).

When I first heard this curse long ago, I understood correctly the first word to be **tōfu** 豆腐 (soybean curd), but I shook my head in doubt and thought, No, that can't be. How could anyone die from hitting his head on the corner of a piece of **tōfu** 豆腐? Maybe it's **tōku no kado** 遠くの角 (a far-off corner). At least, that would make more sense than **tōfu no kado** 豆腐の角. So I misused the expression for a year or two, lending fuel to my growing reputation as a **hen na gaijin** 変な外人 (an oddball foreigner). At last I got it right, but I still wonder how one can die from striking his head against bean curd.

CHAPTER THREE

Use of Living Creatures as Animal Insults

REPTILES AND AMPHIBIANS

There is still lurking in man's subconscious a hostility toward many living creatures. This hostility began when we were not the dominant species on this planet but survived only as frightened nomads in flight from savage four-legged hunters.

Even after the roles were reversed and we became the savage hunters, the old mind-sets—practically instincts—remained, and we continued to distrust and dislike animals. (Hence the hunters' philosophy: If it moves, shoot it!)

To rationalize our instinctive animosity, we attributed to animals unsavory characteristics that were either undeserved or deserved to a lesser degree than popularly believed. We did this also to justify our callous slaughter of other species—to stave off or alleviate our guilt-plagued nightmares. Even in words like nightmare (a female horse that torments us in the night) we can detect this animosity toward animals.

It is likely that most or even all races denigrate other homo sapiens through offensive comparison with animals, fowl, fish, and even insects. In learning Japanese insults based on such comparisons, however, the reader should bear in mind that the characteristics he or she attributes to other species may not be the same as those the Japanese assign to them. Even when the characteristics are the same, there may be a question of degree.

A handy example is the snake. Aside from herpetologists, most Westerners abhor snakes and shudder at their sight. Possibly this hostility harks back in large part to the biblical snake (actually, Satan disguised) which first tempted Eve to sin in the Garden of Paradise. The Japanese have no such myth, which is not to say, however that they love snakes.

Additionally, in the U.S. at least, there are far more danger-ous snakes and in larger numbers than in Japan. The **mamushi** 蝮 and the **habu** ハブ are Japan's only **dokuja** 毒蛇 (poisonous snakes) and except on the pleasant south-ern isles of Amami 奄美, they have never intruded largely into the popular consciousness. Americans, on the other hand, have long been harassed—or so we like to believe— by rattlesnakes, water moccasins, copperheads, and coral snakes. Doubtless, the harm inflicted and the danger pre-sented by these scaly crawlers have been exaggerated (most reptiles, with the exception of the king cobra, fear man as much as we fear them), but we have long belittled people and places we despise through reptilian simile and metaphor; a snake in the grass, the snake pit, cherish a snake in the bosom, and so forth.

But, in Japanese, to compare a person to a snake doesn't carry that much punch, although **Kare wa hebi da** 彼は蛇だ (He's a snake) does suggest a certain degree of cunning.

Aside from that, the only instances that come to mind con-cern the **uwabami** ウワバミ (translated as both boa constric-tor and python) and **dakatsu** 蛇蠍 (snakes and scorpions):

• **uwabami no yō ni nomu**　ウワバミのように飲む
　to drink like a fish (lit., like a python)

**Yūbe uwabami no yō ni o-sake wo nonda kara,
kyō wa futsukayoi de nyūin saseraremasu.**
夕べウワバミのようにお酒を飲んだから、今日は二日
酔いで入院させられます。

I am being hospitalized today with a hangover, because I drank like a fish last night.

Dakatsu no yō ni kirawarete imasu.
蛇蝎のように嫌われています。(He) is despised (lit., hated like snakes and scorpions).

Another reptile that can be used to vilify is the turtle or **kame**, particularly if one says *dongame* 鈍亀 (dull turtle):

Omae no yō na dongame wo yatou to wa yume ni mo omowan zo.
お前のような鈍亀を雇うとは夢にも思わんぞ。
I wouldn't dream of hiring a dull turtle like you.

Then there is **deba-game** 出歯亀 (turtle with buckteeth), which means "a Peeping Tom":

Sono otoko wa deba-game da to wakattara imōto wa zekkō shita.
その男は出歯亀だと判ったら妹は絶交した。
My younger sister broke off with that fellow when she learned he was a Peeping Tom.

MARINE LIFE

Shifting to the finny creatures and their co-dwellers of the deep, let's examine the large variety of comparative disparagements we can find among them. First, the whale:

• **geiin suru** 鯨飲する to drink like a whale

Ojīsan wa maiban Roppongi atari de geiin shimasu. お祖父さんは毎晩六本木辺りで鯨飲します。
Grandfather swills it down every night in Roppongi or thereabouts.

Same 鮫 is a word for shark (**fuka** 鱶 is another), and **same-hada** 鮫肌 describes rough, coarse skin:

tonari no okusan no same-hada　となりの奥さんの
鮫肌　the coarse skin of the wife next-door

Sometimes we see old farming women whose backs are per-
manently rounded from long years of bending over in the
rice paddies. Their backs must have reminded someone of
the curved back of prawns (**kuruma-ebi** 車海老):

- **kuruma-ebi babā**　車海老婆
  old hunch-backed woman

Detarame 出鱈目 is a rather mystifying insult, for its literal translation is "protruding cod eyes," but its actual meaning is "nonsense." The **de** is from **deru** 出る, "to come out,"
while **tara** 鱈 is "cod" and **me** 目 is "eye."

Detarame wo iu na. 出鱈目を言うな。
Don't talk nonsense *or* Tell that to the horse marines.

Kingyo 金魚 means goldfish, while **deme-kin** 出目金 is the
so-called telescope-eye goldfish, a variety with popeyes.
From this word is constructed:

- **deme-kin yarō**　出目金野郎　popeyed fool

Very large mouths remind some of alligators, thus the
expression:

- **wani-guchi** 鰐口 person with a very large mouth
  (lit., alligator mouth)
- **wani-guchi no onna** 鰐口の女　woman with a
  large mouth

A **kappa** 河童 is a mythical river monster that appears in
stories for children:

- **He no kappa.** 屁の河童。It's nothing (lit., It's just
  a river monster passing wind).

This describes something of no value or significance.

The **tengu** 天狗 is another mythical creature, described as a long-nosed goblin. The **tengu** 天狗 is also said to be extremely arrogant, a trait which has given rise to the following expressions:

Shiranakatta no ka. Kare wa fuda-tsuki no tengu da. 知らなかったのか。彼は札付きの天狗だ。
Didn't you know? He's a world-class braggart.
(**Fuda-tsuki** 札付き means to have a label attached.)

- **tengu no yori-ai** 天狗の寄り合い
  assembly of braggarts
- **tengu-banashi** 天狗話 boastful story

Kanojo ni iwaseruto koibito wa Nihon-ichi no kanemochi datte. Tengu-banashi kashira.
彼女に言わせると恋人は日本一の金持ちだって。天狗話かしら。 To hear her tell it, her lover is the richest man in Japan. I wonder if she's just bragging.

- **sukan-tako** すかんたこ disgusting fellow (lit., a disliked octopus)

An na sukan-tako no soba ni iru to gero ga desō da. あんなすかんたこの傍にいるとゲロが出そうだ。
Just being beside him makes my gorge rise.

RATS, RABBITS, AND WEASELS
Nezumi 鼠 is a rat or mouse, while **dobu-nezumi** どぶ鼠 is a gutter rat. A person's morals can be traduced with the use of this scurrilous construction:

- **dobu-nezumi no dōtoku** どぶ鼠の道徳 morals of a gutter rat

Another rather puzzling reference to **nezumi** 鼠 is:

> **atama no kuroi nezumi** 頭の黒い鼠 dishonest ser-
> vant (lit., a black-headed rat).

Is there such a thing as a rat with a black head and body of a different color? Or does the black refer to the color of Japanese hair?

A rabbit-related insult that sprang into the public cognition not long ago was **usagi-goya** 兎小屋, or "rabbit hutch":

> **Nihonjin wa usagi-goya ni sunde iru to iware-mashita.**
> 日本人は兎小屋に住んでいると言われました。
> The Japanese were said to live in rabbit hutches.

If you dislike the way your dinner companion keeps staring at you with black, beady, unblinking eyes, you might say:

> **Itachi no yō na me de mitsumeru na.**
> 鼬のような目で見つめるな。
> Stop staring at me with those beady eyes.

Still another puzzling expression (not really an insult) is:

- **itachi no michi-giri wo suru** 鼬の道切りをする
  to cut off relations with someone (lit., to cut the
  path of a weasel)

INSECTS

Mushi 虫 is the everyday term for insects (or bugs) while the scholarly term is **konchū** 昆虫. **Kemushi** 毛虫 is a cater-pillar and gives us an example of how two cultures view the same object differently. I don't know that many of us would care to cuddle a caterpillar but we certainly don't hold the degree of hostility toward them that the Japanese do. I have heard, however, of one variety of Japanese caterpillar that stings, which may be a contributing factor:

- **kemushi no yō na yatsu** 毛虫のような奴 despicable fellow (lit., someone like a caterpillar)

Other insect-related taunts are:

- **yowa-mushi** 弱虫 weakling (lit., weak bug)
- **hehiri-mushi** 屁ひり虫 small brat (lit., farting insects)
- **mushi-kera** 虫けら scum
- **tentori-mushi** 点取り虫 bookworm (lit., a grade-taking bug)
- **naki-mushi** 泣き虫 crybaby
- **gokiburi teishu** ゴキブリ亭主 a lazy, good-for-nothing husband (**Gokiburi** ゴキブリ means cockroach.)

FOWL

The only offensive remark with feathers on it that comes to mind is **washi-bana** 鷲鼻 or eagle nose:

Sensei, wata(ku)shi no washi-bana wo naosu shujutsu wa arimasen ka.
先生、私の鷲鼻を直す手術はありませんか。
Doctor, isn't there an operation to fix my eagle nose?

FOUR-LEGGED CREATURES

This is an area that produces much pejorative vocabulary. The modifier **yotsu-ashi no** 四足 (four-legged) is sure to wound. And there are others:

- **yotsu-ashi no yabanjin** 四足の野蛮人 bestial barbarian
- **Kono chikushō-me!** この畜生め！ You beast!
- **Konchikushō-me!** こん畜生め！ You brute!
- **Kono kedamono-me!** この獣め！ This animal!

Sonna kōdō wa chikushō no asamashii shirushi da.
そんな行動は畜生の浅ましいしるしだ。
Such behavior is the mark of the beast.

* **yajū** 野獣 a savage beast; a beastly person

Sono hanzai-nin wa yajū da.
その犯罪人は野獣だ。That criminal is a beast.

DOGS AND MONKEYS

The Japanese equivalent of the expression "fight like cats and dogs" is "fight like dogs and monkeys."

Ano futari wa itsumo inu to saru no yō ni kenka wo shite imasu. あの二人はいつも犬と猿のようにけんかをしています。
That pair is always at it like cats and dogs.

Although dogs (**inu** 犬) may be man's best friends, they get their share of verbal knocks in Japan:

* **keisatsu no inu** 警察の狗 a police spy
* **kono inu-me!** この犬め！You dog!
* **inu no tō-boe** 犬の遠吠え useless complaining
  (lit., the barking of a far-away dog)

This refers to a weak person or coward who speaks badly of others behind their backs, without ever coming out and saying what's on his or her mind. Thus, it's like a dog barking at a person or a strong opponent from a safe distance.

* **inu-goroshi** 犬殺し dogcatcher (lit., dog-killer)
  To compare a person to a dogcatcher is sure to get his attention and raise his hackles.
* **inu-zamurai** 犬侍 depraved samurai
* **inu-boneori** 犬骨折 fruitless efforts (lit., dog-bone-breaking)
* **inu-tsukubai** 犬蹲 fawning (lit., dog-crouching)

Westerners tend to think of members of the monkey family as clever, agile, and rather amusing creatures. Although perhaps some Japanese feel similarly, the following three expressions indicate the general feeling is otherwise:

- **saru-mane** 猿真似 copycat (lit., someone who imitates things like a monkey)
- **yamazaru** 山猿 hillbilly (lit., mountain monkey)

Aitsu wa saru da. あいつは猿だ。
He is a cunning, crafty fellow (lit., He's a monkey).

A **hihi** 狒狒 is a dog-faced baboon. By adding **jijī** 爺 (old man) or **babā** 婆 (old woman), we get two very sharp barbs:

- **hihi-jijī** 狒狒爺 dirty old man, lustful old goat, horny geezer (lit., baboonlike old man)
- **hihi-babā** 狒狒婆 lewd old woman (lit., baboon- like old woman)

BADGERS
The badger (**tanuki** 狸) is considered in Japan to be a crafty, rather amusing creature with supernatural powers. It is used in such gibes as:

- **tanuki-jijī** 狸爺 cunning old man
- **tanuki-babā** 狸婆 crafty old woman
- **furu-danuki** 古狸 sly old fox

FOXES
Like a badger, the fox (**kitsune** 狐) is regarded as a wily, crafty, though not so amusing animal:

- **kitsune no yō na kodomo** 狐のような子供 foxy child

Rural Japanese also assigned mystical powers to the fox:

Wakai toki ni sono hito wa kitsune ni tsukareta sō desu. Ima de mo nan to naku okashii yō da.
若い時にその人は狐に憑かれたそうです。今でも何となくおかしいようだ。 It is said that person was possessed by a fox when he was young. Even now there's something strange about him.

COWS

As a field to plow for derisive commentary, cows offer little and can almost be ignored, except for two examples:

- **ushi no yodare no yō** 牛の涎のよう unending, something that drags on (lit., like a cow's saliva)

Bokushi no sekkyō wa ushi no yodare no yō deshita. 牧師の説教は牛の涎のようでした。The preacher's sermon seemed like it would go on forever.

- **ushi-pai** 牛ぱい heavy breasts (The **pai** ぱい comes from **oppai** おっぱい or breasts.)

Kanojo no ushi-pai wa honmono deshō ka.
彼女の牛ぱいは本物でしょうか。
Are her huge breasts real?

CATS

In most cultures, except perhaps that of ancient Egypt, and to a lesser degree, present-day England, **neko** 猫 (house cats) have often received short shrift. Japan is no exception.

- **neko wo kaburu** 猫を被る to pretend to be innocent, to be hypocritical (lit., to put on the cat).
- **neko ni koban** 猫に小判 to cast pearls before swine (lit., gold coins to cats)

- **neko-baba** 猫糞 embezzlement (lit., feline feces) This comes from felines' habit of covering up their business with dirt when they're finished.
- **neko no me no yō ni kawari-yasui** 猫の目のように変わりやすい extremely fickle (lit., changeable as a cat's eyes)
- **neko-pai** 猫ぱい flat-chested (lit., cat tits) Can you imagine any girl so poorly endowed?

Although it is not really an insult, **neko** 猫 is a diminutive colloquialism used to refer to those ladies of the arts called geisha. **Neko wo ireru** 猫を入れる (bring in a cat) means to call in a geisha. Possibly this originated in the use of catgut for the strings of the shamisen geishas often strummed.

OTHER FELINES

If I go out and get sozzled, you can use this expression to describe me:

- **tora ni naru** 虎になる to get blind drunk (lit., to become a tiger)

If the gendarmes collar me, they may take me to a **tora-bako** 虎箱, or drunk tank (lit., tiger box). Such "tigers" can be divided into two groups—the big and the small:

- **ōdora** or **ōtora** 大虎 drunkards (lit., big tigers)
- **kodora** or **kotora** 子虎 drinkers (lit., little tigers)

Shishi 獅子 is an odd word with many meanings, but we are interested here in the one that means "lion":

- **shishi shinchū no mushi** 獅子心中の虫 treacherous friend (lit., an insect in a lion's breast)

Although I unfortunately have had frequent opportunity to make use of this phrase, it is not very common. You may find that only Japanese of a literary bent will know it.

- **shishi-bana** or **shishippana**　獅子鼻　broad, flattish nose

An insult for which one would be long remembered:

Sono hito ni atte hoshii nante, tondemonai! An'na shishi-bana no kebukai yabanjin wa dai kirai yo.
その人に会って欲しいなんて、とんでもない！あんな獅子鼻の毛深い野蛮人は大嫌いよ。
You want me to meet him? Out of the question! I despise that flat-nosed, hairy barbarian.

If you have visited Okinawa, you may recall seeing **kara-shishi** or **kara-jishi** 唐獅子 there. These statues of "lion-dogs," mythical creatures with horrendous faces, usually stand guard in front of temples and tombs. They are called China lions in English.

Buchō no okusan no kao wo mita kai. Kara-jishi mo ii toko da.
部長の奥さんの顔を見たかい。唐獅子もいいとこだ。
Did you see the face of the section-chief's wife?
Even a China lion's face would be an improvement.

- **kara-jishi babā**　唐獅子婆　old woman with a face like a China lion

PIGS
Despite a reportedly rather high level of intelligence, the reputation of the pig suffers from its appearance and perhaps from noisy table manners.

Sono buta no yō na daimyō wa Mito-han no shishi ni ansatsu saremashita. その豚のような大名は水戸藩の志士に暗殺されました。
That swinish **daimyo** was assassinated by patriots of the Mito clan.

This **shishi** 志士 is written with different kanji than the word for lion.

- **tonji** 豚児　my son (lit., pig-child)
- **tonsai** 豚妻　my wife (lit., pig-wife)

BEARS

A freak show in a Japanese circus might display a **kuma-musume** 熊娘, a "bear-girl," or a girl with hair over most of her body.

- **kuma-musume**　熊娘　hairy girl

Hayaku okiru toki, shujin wa kuma mitai yo.
早く起きる時、主人は熊みたいよ。 My husband is like a bear when he gets up early.

The Japanese connotations are the same as the English.

HORSES

Let's look at a sampling of how the Japanese compare horses with people. One reading for the character for horse is **uma** 馬 and another is **ba** 馬.

- **yaji-uma** 野次馬　curious rabble (lit., jeering horses)
- **tsuke-uma wo hiku** 付け馬を曳く　to be followed home by a bill-collector (lit., to lead a trailing horse)
- **doko no uma no hone da ka wakaranai otoko**
  どこの馬の骨だかわからない男　man of doubtful origins, a drifter (lit., horse bones from nobody knows where)
- **iki-uma no me wo nuku yō na otoko** 生き馬の目を抜くような男　a shrewd, very cunning man (lit., a fellow who can steal the eyes out of a living horse)
- **uma no ashi** 馬の脚　poor actor (lit., a horse's leg)
- **uma no mimi ni nembutsu** 馬の耳に念仏　water off a duck's back (lit., a prayer in a horse's ear)

- **baji tōfū** 馬耳東風 unheeded words (lit., an easterly wind in a horse's ears).
- **baka** 馬鹿 fool (lit., a horse-deer)
- **gyūin bashoku suru** 牛飲馬食する to swill and gorge (lit., to drink like a cow and eat like a horse)
- **umazura** 馬面 horse-face
- **jaja-uma** じゃじゃ馬 shrew, virago, termagant (lit., restive horse)

Oyaji to wa uma ga aimasen.
親父とはウマが合いません。 I don't get along with my old man (lit., Our horses don't match).

This need not be insulting, but usually when you don't get along with someone, it is implied that you don't like his words or actions.

MONSTERS, BEASTS, AND FIENDS

Here are some items of virulent vocabulary that malign brutes, devils and inhuman scoundrels:

- **Kono akuma-me!** この悪魔め！ You devil!
- **akuratsu na** 悪辣な cruel and unscrupulous
- **hitode-nashi** 人でなし monster
- **Kono hitode-nashi me!** この人でなしめ （You) brute!
- **nimpinin** 人非人 a brute in human shape
- **chikushō -me** 畜生め （same as above)
- **hakujō na gokudō-me** 薄情な極道め heartless and debauched brute
- **gokudō-yarō** 極道野郎 monstrous villain

Similar words and their usage:

- **hannya no mōshigo** 般若の申し子 demon-child

Uchi no musume ga umareta toki wa sugoku kawaii tenshi da to omotte yorokonda ga, ima ni natte hannya no mōshigo da to wakatta.

うちの娘が生まれたときはすごくかわいい天使だと思って喜んだが、今になって般若の申し子だとわかった。

When our daughter was born, I thought she was a cute little angel, but now I know that she is a demon-child sent by Satan.

• **giri mo ninjō mo nai gokudō-mono**
義理も人情もない極道者 man devoid of all sense of duty and humanity

Sono otoko to wakareta ato kanojo wa giri mo ninjō mo shiranai gokudō-mono to issho ni natta.

その男と別れたあと、彼女は義理も人情もない極道者と一緒になった。After that man and she parted, she took up with a man devoid of any sense of duty and humanity. It serves her right.

• **ningen no kawa wo kabutta chikushō** 人間の皮を被った畜生 an animal in the form of a man

Ojōsan ni ii-nasai yo. Ano otoko wa ningen no kawa wo kabutta chikushō da kara.

お嬢さんに言いなさいよ。あの男は人間の皮を被った畜生だから。Tell your daughter that he's an animal in the form of man.

• **bakemono** 化け物 a spook

Sono akiya ni bakemono ga iru to iu no ka. Omae wa son'na hanashi wo shinjiru noroma ka.

その空家に化け物がいると言うのか。お前はそんな話を信じるのろまか。

You say there are spooks in that vacant house? Are you such a bonehead as to believe that story?

CHAPTER FOUR

Sex, Booze and Money

SEX, IMMORALITY AND MARITAL RELATIONS
The Japanese take a fairly lenient view of sexual indiscretions, but even so there are limits, and people can be quite clear in denouncing excesses.

> **Yujirō wa mainichi te wo komaneite midara na mōsō ni fukette iru yō da ga, nani mo jikkō shinai kara betsu ni fūki wo midashimasen.**
> 裕次郎は毎日手をこまねいて淫らな妄想に耽っているようだが、何も実行しないから別に風紀を乱しません。
> With folded arms Yujirō spends his days lost in lascivious thoughts, but none of his fantasies materialize, so he does no special harm to public morality.

Judging from the frequency in which they are mentioned in literature, Japan has its share of lusty men (**seiyoku no tsuyoi otoko-tachi** 性欲の強い男たち). They are described in such words as:

- **sukebē** 助平 lecher; lecherous
- **sukebē-oni** 助平鬼 lecherous devil, world-class womanizer
- **inran na otoko** 淫乱な男 satyr
- **shikima** 色魔 sex fiend
- **injū** 陰獣 lascivious beast, filthy fiend
- **nikuyoku no gonge** 肉欲の権化 incarnation of carnal desire

Sukebē 助平 is the most often heard of these words, and women may use it when a man tells even a mildly racy joke. It is heard so often that some foreign students mistakenly take it to mean something akin to, "You naughty rascal, you!"

I heard a story (I believe it is not apocryphal) of an eager young American who was sent to join his company's branch in Tokyo. Being a hustler and something of a wag, he had learned a little Japanese to employ in cocktail-party repartee. Laboriously, without the aid of a teacher, he managed to string together a few words in Japanese that he imagined to be equivalent to the English, "Hey, you sly old dog! Getting any new stuff these days?"

Thus far, so good, and at the next martini testimonial given by the gigantic Japanese corporation, which was tied up with the American's company in some commercial arrangement, he sighed the august Mr. Sakimura, the widely respected chairman of the board. Throwing caution to the winds, the young American sashayed up to this forbidding presence and said clearly, **Oi, Sakimura-san, dai-ichi sukebē hanchō-san ja nai ka.** おい、崎村さん、第一助平班長さんじゃないか。 Mr. Sakimura gasped, blanched, and spun on his heels, for the young American had said something like "Hey there, Sakimura, if it isn't just the biggest lecher of them all."

Not long after that, the hapless American was sent home without even the courtesy of a sayonara party.

Bottom line: Don't use **sukebē** 助平 to or about anyone unless you really mean to say he is a lecher ... and not merely a playful old rascal!

I have heard lewd women with whom I consorted say **sukebē-gami** 助平紙 (lecherous paper) to identify the tissue they used to wipe away the aftermath of a sexual encounter. It may be that they use this word more to foreigners than to their fellow countrymen, since **sukebē** 助平 was a word that ninety-nine percent of all American G.I.s in Japan knew and spoke with marked frequency. **Sakura-gami** 桜紙 (cherry paper), on the other hand, was a highly absorbent paper that Japanese women, lewd or not, used to ward off pregnancy.

Japan's **mizu-shōbai** 水商売 ("water business" or nightlife world) has always been fascinating, especially the demimonde. My first direct experience came shortly after World War II in the town of Hachiōji. My two red-blooded comrades and I, on our first night, had found our way unerringly to what we called in my native Texas, with charming delicacy a good-time house.

For nearly three years before that we had been studying the Japanese language and culture from nisei and kibei teachers. These instructors had filled our eager ears with stories about the marvels of Japan's **karyū-kai** 花柳界 (flower-and-willow world), so we had salivated lustily awaiting this night.

Even the terminology bespoke the wonders to which we would be treated. Flower-and-willow world, indeed! And those who toiled among the flowers and willows were called by such names as **baishumfu** 売春婦 (a woman who sells spring) and **baishō-fu** 売笑婦 (a woman who sells laughter). Even the establishment where they awaited us horizontal on their workbenches was called a **baishun-yado** 売春宿 (inn that sells spring). Less fancy nomenclature includes:

- **akasen chiiki** 赤線地域 red-light district (lit., redline area)
- **kōtō no chimata** 紅灯の巷 gay quarters
- **imbai-yado** 淫売宿 brothel, cat house
- **jorō-ya** 女郎屋 whorehouse, sporting house

Anyway, it would have been more fitting if our teachers had taught us yet another word for the business of prostitution, namely, **doromizu kagyō** 泥水稼業. Its meaning, "muddy-water profession," would have been far more appropriate to the dirty, plain girls with runny noses who were paraded before us that evening just before we fled into the night.

A Southern gentleman once greeted his guest, who was just descending from a train, with the words, "Wal suh, shall we indulge in a mint julep first or proceed direct to the hoah house?" In similar spirit, you might ask your Japanese guest for the evening:

> **Sā, ippai nomō ka. Sore tomo yūjo-machi ni chokusetsu ikō ka.**
> さあ、一杯飲もうか。それとも遊女街に直接行こうか。
> Well, shall we have a drink? Or should we go direct-ly to the district of playful women?

Women who deal in spring are also called those who "play" (**asobu** 遊ぶ). Another reading of the character for **asobu** 遊ぶ is **yu** 遊, which gives us the following three words for a red-light district:

- **yūjo-machi** 遊女街
- **yūri** 遊里
- **yūkaku** 遊郭

Other such vocabulary items are:

- **iro-zato** 色里 gay quarters (lit., color-village)
- **iro-machi** 色街 gay quarters (lit., color-town)
- **fuyajō** 不夜城 gay quarters (lit., castle of no night)
- **girō** 妓楼 brothel

Reminiscent of mothers who called Hell "the bad place," a few Japanese of Victorian bent referred to those areas that market springtime (**haru wo hisagu** 春をひさぐ) as:

- **yokunai tokoro** 良くない所 bad place
- **yokaranu basho** 良からぬ場所 (same as above but slightly more literary in tone)

The managers and pimps go by a variety of names, **pombiki** ぽん引き and **ponchan** ぽんちゃん being the basic two. Also, we have:

- **himo** ひも
- **gyūtarō** 妓夫太郎／牛太郎

The business of dealing in human flesh (what in the West is called white slavery) is **jinshin baibai** 人身売買, while a person engaging in this sordid trade is a **hito-kai** 人買い (lit., person-buyer) or a fleshmonger. **Yarite-babā** 遣り手婆 can be used to mean a procuress.

Women who sell their bodies (**mi wo uru** 身を売る) can be called any of the following, which all basically mean prostitute. The following first four terms specifically refer to a streetwalker:

- **shūgyōfu** 醜業婦
- **gaishō** 街娼
- **yotaka** 夜鷹 (lit., night hawk)
- **jorō** 女郎
- **pampan** パンパン
- **pansuke** パン助
- **baita** 売女
- **imbai** 淫売
- **machi no onna** 街の女 (lit., woman of the town)
- **yami no onna** 闇の女 (lit., woman of the darkness)

Nido to sono baita wo kono uchi ni irenai kara oboete oke. 二度とその売女をこの家に入れないから覚えておけ。Just remember, I'm never again letting that slut in this house.

Some of these terms of defamation can be quite flowery. For instance:

- **machi no tenshi** 街の天使 (lit., angel of the town)
- **yami no hana** 闇の花 (lit., flower of the darkness)
- **tsukimi-sō** 月見草 (lit., primrose)

Or they can be crudely direct, such as:

- **doya-pan** どやパン flophouse slut
- **shōgi** 娼妓/倡伎 licensed prostitute

Loose women have not quite crossed the line into professionalism are given such names as:

- **inran na onna** 淫乱な女 lewd woman
- **bakuren onna** 莫連女 abandoned woman, gutter trull
- **ikagawashii onna** いかがわしい女 woman of ill repute
- **jidaraku onna** 自堕落女 woman of uncertain reputation (I could never really understand what was uncertain or dubious about the reputation of these women. After all, a whore is a whore.)
- **ama** あま slut, bitch
- **hasuppa na musume** 蓮っ葉な娘 wanton girl
- **shirigaru onna** 尻軽女 woman sho sleeps around (lit., a woman with light hips that are easy moved from **futon** to **futon**.

An apprentice geisha is a **maiko** 舞妓 (alas, a dying breed). When she becomes a full-fledged **geisha** or **geiko** (**ippon ni naru** 一本になる), she lost her virginity to a high-bidding customer in a ceremony called **mizuage-shiki** 水揚げ式. **Mizuage** 水揚げ means to land fish or to lift fish from the water. The connection between hoisting a netload of fish onto land and the defloration of a **maiko** 舞妓 is not clear. Perhaps it is better that way.

In any event, the **geisha** (some prefer the word **geiko** 芸妓) may thereafter change bed partners often or may remain faithful to one patron for many years. She may even take a lover (students are prime candidates) on whom she lavishes gifts and gelt. Whatever form her **futon** 布団 fun takes, however, the true **geisha** is not usually thought of as a whore, although some do sink to that level. Such are called:

- **korobi-geisha** 転び芸者 (roll-over **geisha**)
- **imosuke** 芋助 (potato gal)
- **daruma-geisha** 達磨芸者 (lit., round-bottomed **geisha**) This term comes from the **daruma** 達磨 doll, which rolls over easily but always regains a vertical position.
- **sanryū-geisha** 三流芸者 (third-class **geisha**)
- **shomben-geisha** 小便芸者 (piss **geisha**)
- **haori-geisha** 羽織芸者 **geisha** wearing a **haori** 羽織 coat (A true **geisha** would never wear a **haori** 羽織.)

During periods of hostility and armed tension, girls called **ian-fu** 慰安婦 (girls with no elastic in their drawers) were dispatched to combat areas to comfort the boys. Most of this comforting was carried on silently in a horizontal position.

An older term for chippy that one may still come across is **keisei** 傾城, as in the proverb:

Keisei ni makoto nashi. 傾城に誠なし。
There is no truth in the words of a whore.

At one time in Japan's colorful past, a species of doxy must have loitered in or around the public bathhouses (**sentō** 銭湯). These bathhouse prostitutes were called **yuna** 湯女, and thereby hangs a tale.

When then President Ronald Reagan visited Japan and addressed the Diet, he essayed a short sentence in Japanese. My guess is that he intended to say, **Nichibei no yūkō wa eien desu** 日米の友好は永遠です, or "Japanese-American friendship is forever."

I was listening to the speech on satellite television with several native speakers of Japanese, including the incumbent Mrs. Seward, who thought that what Reagan had said in his poorly enunciated Japanese was, **Nichibei no yuna wa taihen desu** 日米の湯女は大変です, which would have meant something like, "Japanese-American bathhouse prostitutes are a real handful."

My wife, being of a literal turn of mind, immediately sang out, "I wonder how he found that out so quickly. He's only been in Japan two days."

Less direct ways of referring to those of wonderously easy virtue whom the French call **filles de joie** (women of joy) are:

- **ichiya-zuma** 一夜妻 （wife for one night）

Pamma パンマ is a tart who doubles as a masseuse. Once, years ago, an American friend stayed in a hotel with the tell-tale sign of the **sakasa-kurage** 逆さ海月, upside-down jelly-fish, outside. Getting settled in, he asked the front desk to send up a masseuse. Signals must have gotten mixed, because when the woman arrived, it soon became apparent that the service the American wanted was not the one the woman intended to provide. To the woman's exasperation my friend kept insisting that she rub him down, so finally she drew herself up proudly and announced in ringing tones, "Me no masseuse. Me whore!"

Another word with the same meaning as the above **pamma** パンマ is **nadekko-san** 撫でっ子さん, whose provenance is complicated. **Naderu** 撫でる is the verb for "to stroke, fondle, or caress," and from the same character comes **nadeshiko** 撫子—a flower called a pink. The name of this flower is also used in the expression **Yamato nadeshiko** 大和撫子, or a "traditional daughter of Japan." Since a **Yamato nadeshiko-san** 大和撫子さん is at the other end of the social scale from a **nadekko-san** 撫でっ子さん, it must have been somewhat of a cynic who dreamed it up.

Sometimes a distinction must be made between a hooker who serves Japanese men and one who spread joy among Westerners. **Wapan** 和パン is the former, and **yōpan** 洋パン and **yōshō** 洋娼 are both names for the latter.

While not a prostitute, of course, a Japanese woman who lives with a Westerner is called an **onri** オンリ, or "only" ("I speak true. You are only one").

Let me interrupt this rather lengthy listing of Japanese words for prostitute to remind the reader that there is also a cornucopia of such terms of disparagement in English: trollop, fallen woman, floozie, slut, trull, hustler, drab, hooker, bin, ten-penny slut, call-girl, street walker, bawd, doxy, lady of the evening, demirep. I have even heard such women referred to as "Mrs. Warren."

Moving up in the professional world, we encounter the corresponding expressions for the higher-class prostitute:

- **pro no onna** プロの女 (This means a woman of the profession, while a **hai-puro** ハイプロ, or "high-pro" is a high-class bestower of joyful laughter.)

From days past come three words meaning prostitute that are rooted in Japanese culture:

- **shiro-kubi** 白首 (lit., white-neck; from the powdered necks and low nape-lines of dancers, serving girls, and geisha)

- **shira-byōshi** 白拍子 (This comes from the term for the promiscuous dancing girls who performed in traveling troupes and kept up the rhythm of the music with white clappers called **hyōshi** 拍子.)

- **bikuni** 比丘尼 (The primary dictionary definition is a Buddhist priestess but a secondary meaning from the Edo period is a low-class prostitute dressed as a nun. Further inquiries, however, reveal there was a time in Japanese history when Buddhist nuns of a certain sect roamed the countryside begging alms for their home-temple and offering sexual favors to the hesitant as a persuasive device. Mnemonic: a **bikuni** 比丘尼 in a bikini).

Rashamen ラシャ綿 is another word from the past that is nonetheless familiar to most Japanese. It means "a foreigner's mistress," and the charm of the word lies in its origin. **Rasha** ラシャ is a kind of wool cloth, and **men** is short for **menyō** 綿羊, or "sheep." This wool cloth was imported into Japan by some resident Westerners (perhaps Dutchmen), and, in time, the people of Nagasaki began to nickname Westerners **rasha** ラシャ.

Then some people chanced to look into the bedrooms of these **rasha** ラシャ, where much to their amazement, sheep appeared to be asleep on several of the beds ... with Western men. Always ready to believe any outlandish story about the hairy barbarians, the natives concluded that the Westerners had an excessive fondness for barnyard creatures and were keeping ewes for fun and erotic relaxation. Such sheep were called **rasha no menyō** ラシャの綿羊 (a foreigner's sheep), which came to be shortened to **rashamen** ラシャ綿.

At last, the Japanese got a closer look into those bedrooms and discovered to their dismay that what they had fondly imagined to be sheep were nothing more than large dogs sleeping at their masters' feet. By then, however, the word **rashamen** ラシャ綿 was already in use, so when Japanese women replaced the dogs in foreign beds, the derisive appellation transferred to them.

In Japan, honest lust is one thing, whole perversion (**hentai seiyoku** 変態性欲) is quite another. Deviates are usually described with the adjective **etchi na** エッチな, which approximates the **h** sound in **hentai seiyoku** 変態性欲. A rank degenerate could also be called a **henshitsu-sha** 変質者.

A classic usage of the terms was seen in 1936 in the murder trial of the infamous Miss Sada Abe. Sada and her lover had been shacked up for several days in an inn in Tokyo's Arakawa Ward. There they had engaged in a sex marathon that shocked even the hardened maids of that "hot pillow" inn. Being a **rinki-onna** 悋気女 (jealous woman), Sada hated the thought of her paramour returning to the arms of his wife when their tryst ended. She did not want to share him (or his equipment) with anyone, so while he was asleep she cut off the poor devil's unit with a kitchen knife, after which he bled to death. To cap her hard night's work, Sada carved a line of **kanji** on Kichizo's thigh. It read, **Sada Kichi futari** 定·吉二人, "Sada and Kichi, the two of us."

At her trial, the prosecution considered charging Miss Sada with being a **hentai seiyoku-sha** 変態性欲者 (sexual pervert) but at last relented and changed the wording of the charge to **ijōseiyoku-sha** 異常性欲者 (an oversexed person). Sada smilingly admitted to the latter term—it was the former that had outraged her. "Sexual pervert, indeed!"

One night, I chanced to enter a restaurant and found a Japanese acquaintance of mine quarreling with a woman who turned out to be his mistress. He saw me and asked that I join them at their table. He then introduced the woman as **Yarase no Michiko** やらせの美知子. This broke me up, for **yaraseru** やらせる is a verb for "to let do." Meaning? "This is Michiko who lets anyone do it with her."

When a Japanese husband starts to openly engage in extramarital exploits, he is said to be a **fuda-tsuki no uwaki-mono** 札付きの浮気者, or "infamous womanizer" (lit., philanderer with a label attached). Thereupon, the man's wife may begin to burn with jealousy and can be said to be a **yaki-mochi-yaki** 焼き餅焼き, or "grilled rice cakes." Rice cakes (**mochi** 餅) are heated (**yaku** 焼く) in the hottest flames of a charcoal fire. It is the intensity of these flames that is likened to the passion of jealousy.

If a woman's complaints drive her husband to desperate measures, he may become a **gokudō teishu** 極道亭主 (rotten, filthy brute) and his wife may refer to him in such scathing words as **uchi no gokudō** うちの極道 (my brute or the brute of our house). She might also call him **uchi no nora** (my stray).

On the other hand, if the wife has become the domineering one in the family, **kakā denka** 嬶天下 (petticoat government) can be said to be the form of administration governing their domestic lives. She will have become a **Kampaku**

Nyōbō (bossy wife), and he a **nyōbō kōkō no teishu** (a uxorious hasband).

Tanabe-san no uchi wa kakā denka da. Kare wa itsumo nyōbō no shiri ni shikarete iru.
田辺さんのうちは嚊天下だ。彼はいつも女房の尻に敷かれている。Mr. Tanabe is a hen-pecked husband; he is always at his wife's beck and call (lit., spread out like a cushion under his wife's hips).

To continue the tale of Tanabe:

Tanabe-san takes to strong drink and gets swacked as often as he can afford. With his **nomi-nakama** 飲み仲間 (saloon cronies), he frequents a ginmill called the Bar Madrid. The first night he and his **doraku-nakama** 道楽仲間 (fellow profligates) went there, the **Mama-san** ママさん (bar manageress) asked their names. Tanabe introduced each of the four as:

- **Yopparai-san** 酔っ払いさん Mr. Drunkard
- **Nondakure-san** 飲んだくれさん Mr. Sot
- **Yoidore-san** 酔いどれさん Mr. Topper
- **Hidari-kiki-san** 左利きさん Mr. Lush

Mama-san laughed and asked Tanabe-san's name. In unison, the four cried, **Hidari-uchiwa-san** 左団扇さん!

Literally, **hidari-uchiwa** 左団扇 means "left fan" or, by slight extension, a fan that is held in the left hand. The expression can also refer to a man who enjoys a good, idle life while living off the earnings of his daughter or wife.

In this case, Mrs. Tanabe was a hard-working teacher, while her **sodai-gomi** 粗大ゴミ (outsized garbage) of a husband seemed to be forever unemployed.

Why a fan held in the left hand? To keep the right hand free to pour and drink sake, of course.

Later, Mrs. Tanabe calls the Bar Madrid and talks to **Mama-san**:

Tanabe: **Tanabe desu ga, uchi no sodai-gomi wa guden-guden ni yotte iru deshō ka.**
田辺ですが、うちの粗大ゴミはぐでんぐ でんに酔っているでしょうか。
Is my pile of garbage there and is he already snockered?

Mama-san: **Ee, Jitsu wa.** ええ、実は。
Well, the truth is ...

Tanabe: (her voice has become strident): **Sō omotta wa. Sate, sono dōraku-mono wo denwa ni yonde kudasai.** そう思ったわ。さて、 その道楽者を電話に呼んでください。
I thought as much. Well, call that liber- tine to the phone.

Mama-san: **Chotto muzukashii wa ne. Yuka no ue de yoitsuburete imasu kara.**
ちょっと難しいわね。床の上で酔いつぶ れていますから。 That may be a little hard to do. He's passed out on the floor.

MONEY

It is called **okane** お金 as well as: **kinken** 金銭, **tsūka** 通貨, **shihei** 紙幣, **kahei** 貨幣, **genkin** 現金. Those of us who hate to part with even a small amount of it are called:

- **nigiri-ya** 握り屋 tight-fisted person
- **gametsui hito** がめつい人 miser
- **shimittare** しみったれ tightwad
- **ichimon-oshimi** 一文惜しみ skinflint
- **rinshoku-jijī** 吝嗇爺 scrooge

**Uchi no danna wa totemo kane-banare ga warui
wa yo.** うちの旦那はとても金離れが悪いわよ。
My husband is very close-fisted.

**Utchi no wa motto yo. Sukoburu-tsuki no kechim-
bō yo.** うちのはもっとよ。すこぶる付きのケチん坊よ。
Mine is worse. He is a notorious penny pincher.

Stinginess is related to greed (**yokubari** 欲張り). Relevant
expressions are:

- **don-yoku** 貪欲 (same as above)

Kimi no don-yoku wa taishita mon da.
君の貪欲は大したもんだ。
Your greed really overwhelms me.

- **yokubari-babā** 欲張り婆 greedy old woman
- **haikin-shugi** 拝金主義 worship of money (or the
  god Mammon)
- **shusendo** 守銭奴 money-grubber

Those of the opposite persuasion (like my irresponsible
daughter) toss their money to the winds like grain. They are
called **rōhika** 浪費家 or spendthrifts.

**Uchi no musume wa yumizu no yō ni kane wo
tsukau.** うちの娘は湯水のように金を使う。
My daughter spends money like water. (**Yumizu** 湯
水 means hot and cold water.)

Sooner or later the spendthrifts fall heir to **kinketsu-byō** 金
欠病 (lit., shortage-of-money sickness). They become:

- **monnashi** 文無し deadbeats
- **okera** オケラ penniless persons

They begin to bum off (**takaru** たかる) their friends. If it is my wanton daughter, she may come home as a shin-gnawer (**sune-kajiri** 脛かじり) and sponge off her old man. When I see her, I think:

Shakkin ga kimono wo kite aruite iru yō na mon da. 借金が着物を着て歩いているようなもんだ。
She is like borrowed money walking around with a kimono on.

She'll tell me spitefully:

Otōsan wa kechi-kechi shite iru kara, sugu soko no shichiya ni itte okane wo kariru wa.
お父さんはけちけちしているから、すぐそこの質屋に行ってお金を借りるわ。
Because you're such a skinflint, I'll just go to that pawn shop down the street and borrow some money.

and I'll reply:

Ano iji-kitanai jijī ka. Yoshita hō ga ii zo. Kare wa moji-dōri no kyūketsuki da. あの意地汚い爺か。止した方がいいぞ。彼は文字通りの吸血鬼だ。
That swinish old man? You'd better give up that idea. He's a veritable bloodsucker.

CHAPTER FIVE

Mind and Mouth

VOICES AND WORDS

Voices may be soft and soothing, or they may grate on your nerves.

- **kasure-goe** かすれ声 hoarse voice
- **shagare-goe** 嗄れ声 grating, raucous voice

It may be a shrill voice, or **kiiroi koe** 黄色い声 (lit., a yellow voice), or one that is offensive to the ears (**mimi-zawari** 耳障り).

Sono mimi-zawari na koe wa mō takusan da.
その耳障りな声はもうたくさんだ。
I just can't stand that rasping voice anymore.

As in English, a nasal voice (**hana ni kakatta koe** 鼻に掛かった声) is one that whines:

Saburō wa asa kara hana ni kakatta koe de nakigoto wo itte iru.
三郎は朝から鼻に掛かった声で泣き言を言っている。
Saburo starts with his whining complaints in the morning.

Nakigoto 泣き言, "crying things," are complaints.

A **gami-gami onna** がみがみ女 is a shrew while a **gami-gami-babā** がみがみ婆 is an old shrew. To be especially merciless we can add the verb **hoeru** 吠える (to bark):

Uchi ni kaettara kami-san wa sugu gami-gami hoe-dashita.
うちに帰ったらカミサンはすぐがみがみ吠え出した。
As soon as I got home, my old lady started her noisy fault-finding (**Hoe-dasu** 吠え出す means to start barking.)

When a person's words make no sense at all, we can characterize them by saying:

- **gu ni mo tsukan koto** 愚にもつかん事 terrible nonsense, absolute tommyrot
- **chōkō-zetsu** 長広舌 long-windedness (The characters stand for long, wide tongue.)

Nakasone-san no chōkō-zetsu ni aki-aki shite shimaimashita.
中曽根さんの長広舌に飽き飽きしてしまいました。
I grew tired of listening to Mr. Nakasone's long-windedness.

Kare no gu ni mo tsukan kurigoto wa zenzen suji ga tōtte imasen.
彼の愚にもつかん繰言は全然筋が通っていません。
His ridiculous ramblings make no sense at all.

Three withering sentences to effectively blacken someone's ability in Japanese are:

Taitei no Amerika no gaikōkan wa nihongo no ni no ji mo shirimasen. 大抵のアメリカの外交官は日本語のにの字も知りません。

Most American diplomats do no know one word of Japanese (lit., don't even know the **kanji** from the **ni** に in **nihongo** 日本語).

• **hana-mochi naranai** 鼻持ちならない intolerable; detestable (lit., the nose can't bear it)

Karera no nihongo wa hana-mochi narimasen.
彼らの日本語は鼻持ちなりません。
Their Japanese stinks.

Karera no nihongo wa tende sama ni narimasen.
彼らの日本語はてんで様になりません。
Their Japanese is lousy.

When we focus on English, we find:

Eigo no ei no ji mo shiranai.
英語の英の字も知らない。
(He) doesn't know any English at all.

• **susamajii eigo** 凄まじい英語 terrible English
• **shafu eigo** 車夫英語 pidgin English, kitchen English

This is an older expression. **Shafu** 車夫 means rickshaw puller. Rickshaw pullers spoke neither refined nor correct English, if they spoke any at all.

A port jargon called the Yokohama dialect could be heard in the 1860s and 1870s. Its practitioners said **Walk allimasu** for **Wakarimasu** 分かります (I understand), among other depravities. These deficients also used expressions like the following:

• **coots pon pon** bootmaker (**Kutsu** 靴 are shoes or boots and **pon pon** is bang bang.)

- **okee aboneye pon pon** big dangerous earthquake
(**Okee** is **ōkii** 大きい or "big"; **aboneye** is **abunai**
危ない, or "dangerous"; and **pon pon** is "bang
bang" for "earthquake.")

Japanese who learned enough English to become fairly adequate interpreters and translators were often looked down upon by other Japanese, who called them **eigo-zukai** 英語使い, or "English-users." This name seems harmless enough in English, but in Japanese it is definitely pejorative.

Broken English can be expressed as **katakoto-majiri no eigo** 片言交じりの英語, as in:

**Ra Mōru no mama-san wa, boku no kao wo miru
nari katakoto-majiri no susamajii eigo wo
hanashi-hajimeru.** ラモールのママさんは、僕の顔
を見るなり片言交じりの凄まじい英語を話し始める。
As soon as the Mama-san at the bar Rat Mort sees my
face, she starts speaking in terribly broken English.

If a person's **kanji** and **kana** are written in a slovenly hand, we may call him or her a **sho ga tsutanai hito** 書が拙い人. Such words are quite hurtful in Japan, where people take much pride in the quality of their handwriting. (**Sho** 書 is the **on** reading for the character meaning to write.)

MENTAL CAPACITY

The Japanese have been fairly inventive in devising words that cast shadows on the function and the contents of minds. There are so many ways to say that someone is a meathead or half-wit that I can list only the more common here. Unless otherwise noted, they all carry the clear message that the person under fire is a knucklehead and maybe even chicken-witted to boot:

- **tonchiki-me** 頓痴気め (lit., dull and foolish in spirit)

Kono tonchiki yarō-me! Totto-to dete ike!
この頓痴気野郎め！とっと出て行け！
Get out of here, you fool!

- **hiru-andon** 昼行灯 (lit., a day-time night lamp; in other words, someone as stupid as a lamp that burns in the bright of day)
- **tōhenboku** 唐変木 (lit., a Chinese-changing stick.) The etymology is unclear.
- **wakarazu-ya** 分からず屋 thick-headed person

Kono kyōshitsu niwa wakarazu-ya bakari dakara sensei wa hara wo kiru tokoro da. この教室には分からず屋ばかりだから先生は腹を切る所だ。
Because there is nothing but dolts in this classroom, the teacher is about to commit **hara-kiri.**

- **ahō** 阿呆 dumb ass (This is as often heard as **baka** 馬鹿 but has a somewhat gentler sound.)
- **manuke** 間抜け dimwit (lit., out of place)
- **gubutsu** 愚物 foolish chucklehead
- **usunoro** うす鈍 feeble-witted
- **tawake-mono** 戯け者 dunce (**Tawakeru** 戯ける is a verb meaning to talk foolishly while **mono** 者 is "person.")
- **nō-nashi** 能無し brainless

Ano nō-nashi to kekkon shita no ga somo-somo no machigai da wa to iinagara obasan wa naite imashita. あの能無しと結婚したのがそもそもの間違いだわと言いながら叔母さんは泣いていました。
Sobbing, my aunt said that her first mistake was to have married such a know-nothing.

- **baka** 馬鹿 fool
- **ō-baka** 大馬鹿 great fool
- **noroma** のろま dummy
- **anpontan** あんぽんたん simpleton

Kono anpontan-me! Hira-shain no bunzai de namaiki ja nai ka. このあんぽんたんめ！平社員の分際で生意気じゃないか。
You simpleton! You're impertinent for a mere clerk.

- **o-medetai** 御目出度い scatterbrain

Medetai 目出度い by itself means congratulatory but with the prefix **o-** 御 it means someone not playing with a full deck of cards.

Omae no kareshi wa o-medetai yatsu bakari da.
お前の彼氏は御目出度い奴ばかりだ。
Your boyfriends are all morons.

- **tansai-bō** 単細胞 guy who is short on talent
- **tomma** 頓馬 (lit., a dull horse.)
- **kabocha** カボチャ cabbage head (lit., pumpkin head)

The word **baka** 馬鹿 can be intensified with precedents like these:

- **origami-tsuki no baka** 折り紙付きの馬鹿 acknowledged fool
- **shōshin shōmei no baka** 正真正銘の馬鹿 downright fool
- **sokonuke no baka** 底抜けの馬鹿 out-and-out fool (lit., bottomless fool)
- **akireta baka** 呆れた馬鹿 hopeless dingbat

- **kamaboko-baka** 蒲鉾馬鹿 (lit., fish-cake fool; a fool pinned to a board like a fish cake)
- **tanjun-baka** 単純馬鹿 simple nitwit
- **usura-baka** うすら馬鹿 trifle wanting in the brain department, dumbshit
- **ō-baka Santarō** 大馬鹿三太郎 big dolt Santaro (like the television character)

All of the following also accuse the target being disparaged of stupidity:

- **gūtara** ぐうたら addlepated loafer
- **gujin** 愚人 ninny
- **oroka-mono** 愚か者 harebrained
- **bonyari-mono** ぼんやり者 absent-minded person

Sono bonyari-mono no Saburō wa mata kuru no wo wasureta.
そのぼんやり者の三郎はまた来るのを忘れた。That absent-minded Saburo has forgotten to come again.

- **nukesaku** 抜け作 bonehead (lit., with the makings left out)
- **toroi yatsu** とろい奴 sluggish dolt
- **shiremono** 痴れ者 dunderhead
- **yotarō** 与太郎 ignoramus (**Yota** 与太 is nonsense and **rō** 郎 is fellow.)
- **ahondara** 阿呆陀羅 (あほんだら) yo-yo (This word probably comes from **ahodara-kyō** 阿呆陀羅経, a parody on a Buddhist sutra.)

Seijika wa mina yoku ga fukai ahondara de komaru. 政治家は皆欲が深い阿呆陀羅で困る。It is frustrating that the politicians are all greedy yo-yos.

- **nō-tarin**　脳たりん　short on brains
- **o-hitoyoshi**　お人好し　naive isimpleton
- **o-tenten**　おてんてん　feather-brained

Tenten てんてん is the word to describe something floating around like a feather.

- **o-tsumu-tenten**　おつむてんてん　(essentially the same meaning as above. **O-tsumu** おつむ is a children's word for head.)
- **boya-boya shita hito**　ぼやぼやした人　absent-minded goose

Sono boya-boya shita hisho wo hayaku kubi ni shinai to akaji ga deru yo. そのぼやぼやした秘書を早く首にしないと赤字がでるよ。
If you don't fire that absent-minded secretary soon, we'll go into the red.

You may come across these as well:

- **toppoi yatsu**　とっぽい奴　someone a little weird in the head, cuckoo
- **Nihon onchi**　日本音痴　someone who knows nothing at all about Japan
- **sempaku chishiki**　浅薄知識　superficial knowledge
- **nameru**　嘗める　to make a fool of
- **mono-oboe ga warui**　物覚えが悪い　to be slow-witted, a slow learner
- **donkan na baita**　鈍感な売女　stupid whore
- **atama ga usui**　頭が薄い　dumb (lit., thin head)
- **atama ga karui**　頭が軽い　dumb (lit., light head)
- **Kono do-ahō.**　この ド阿呆。You dunce.
- **nō-miso ga kusatta yatsu**　脳味噌が腐った奴　person with rotten brains, ignoramus

The following illustrate usage:

- **Tawakeru na.** 戯けるな Stop playing the fool.
- **Yabo na koto wo kiku na.** 野暮な事を訊くな。
  Don't ask me stupid questions.
- **gariben suru** ガリ勉する to plug away

Sono seinen wa gariben na no ni igai ni gigochinai bunshō wo kakun da. その青年はガリ勉なのに意外にぎごちない文章を書くんだ。
Although that youth is very industrious (at school), he writes very awkward sentences.

- **shō-gakkō chūtai** 小学校中退 grade-school dropout
- **hana-hojikuri** 鼻穿り nose-picker

Namaiki ja nai ka. Kono shō-gakkō chūtai no hana-hojikur-me ga.
生意気じゃないか。この小学校中退の鼻穿りめが。
You are very impudent for a nose-picking grade-school dropout!

- **noroma** のろま nincompoop, dummy

Kimi wa yoppodo no noroma da nā.
君はよっぽどののろまだなあ。
You really are quite a nincompoop, you know.

- **baka-banashi** 馬鹿話 drivel

Omae no baka-banashi wa mō takusan da.
お前の馬鹿話はもう沢山だ。
I've had enough of your drivel.

- **kokoroe-chigai** 心得違い misguided
- **baka na baita** 馬鹿な売女 ignorant slut

Jein omae wa kokoroe-chigai no baka na baita da.
ジェインお前は心得違いの馬鹿な売女だ。
Jane, you're a misguided, ignorant slut.

**Jiten de baka to iu kotoba wo hiite mireba omae
no shashin ga notteru zo.** 辞典で馬鹿という言葉を
引いて見ればお前の写真が載ってるぞ。
If you look up the word **baka** 馬鹿 in a dictionary,
you'll find your photograph there.

Sometimes the origins of these words of execration will help
to lodge them more firmly in your memory:

- **keikōto** 蛍光灯 slow to catch on (lit., a fluorescent
  lamp)
- **tempo-sen** 天保銭 simpleton (lit., a coin on the
  Tempo era [1830-33] not worth even a **sen** 銭
  today in actual monetary value)
- **sukotari** 少足り lacking a little upstairs (**suko** 少
  from **sukoshi** 少し, "little," and **tari** 足り from
  tarinai 足りない, 'to be lacking')

Beyond simple stupidity lies actual pathological mentality
and even insanity. **Kichigai** 気違い is the most common
word for insane. Also:

- **hakuchi** 白痴 idiot
- **ki ga furete iru** 気が狂れている simple simon,
  addlepated
- **hidari-maki** 左巻き (Perhaps 'eccentric' is closer
  to the true meaning, literally, 'wound left.')
- **teinōji** 低脳児 idiot child
- **kurukuru-pā** くるくるパー touched in the head
  (This was popularized by Mr. Tony Tani, a TV
  comedian of the 1960s.)
- **Kono kichigai-me!** この気違いめ！ You moron!

- **boke** ぼけ befuddled
- **Nihon-boke** 日本ぼけ befuddled mental condition that comes from long residence in Japan.

As pointed out elsewhere, a great many words in Japanese cannot be translated into English precisely. To enjoy their full favor, we must rely on figurative instead of literal interpretations. **Berammē** べらんめえ is such a word:

- **berammē kotoba wo tsukau**
  べらんめえ言葉を使う to use rough, vulgar speech (most often refers to the speech of gangsters and other flotsam of the streets of Tokyo)

Characteristics of **berammē** べらんめえ speech are the substitution of **e** for **a** and the rolled **r**. Instead of **Yatsu no bero wa shiroku-nai ja nai ka** 奴のべろは白くないじゃないか (Can't you see that his tongue is not white?), an Asakusa pimp would be more likely to say, **Yatsu no berro wa shiroku-nei ja nei ka** 奴のべろは白くねいじゃねいか.

Closely related, in sound at least, to **berammē** べらんめえ is **berabō** べら棒, which means 'terrible.'

- **berabō na hito-de** べらぼうな人出 an awful lot of people
- **berabō ni isogu** べらぼうに急ぐ to be in a terrible hurry
- **Berabō-me!** べらぼうめ！ Confound it!

Nani wo iu no ka kono berabō-me.
何を言うのかこのべらぼうめ 。 I'll see you in hell.

CHAPTER SIX

Origin, Status, and Employment

ORIGINS

In Japanese society, much attention is paid to where you come from and what your role (**hombun** 本分) is. Because origin and position are so important, they are often referred to when belittling others. This is sometimes accomplished through the speaker's choice of pronouns, verbs, and verb endings, the choice of which will show respect or contempt, or denigration is achieved by the judicious use of words of debasement.

Take the words identifying provincial people as examples. Such words clearly reflect the dichotomy between city and rural cultures. Americans, or example, have always poked fun at rural folk, calling them hayseeds or hillbillies. It is acknowledged, nonetheless, that lives of culture and sophistication may be led away from the metropolitan turmoil and clamor. Persons of wealth and refinement do occasionally seek out the quieter and more sedate existence vouchsafed by the countryside.

Not so in Japan. If a city **bunka-jin** 文化人 (man of culture) does retire to the hinterlands, it is only in search of affordable housing in which to spend his declining years.

True, there are many **inaka no narikin** 田舎の成金 (rural nouveaux riches) these days who are using their new land-based wealth to travel abroad and acquire samples of the beaux-arts. In the fullness of time, this may ameliorate the contempt with which rustics are viewed, but that day has not yet dawned. Regard how disdain for the country dwellers is manifested in words:

- **inakappe** 田舎っぺ country oaf
- **inaka-kusai** 田舎臭い backward (lit., stinking of the country)
- **yamadashi** 山出し yokel (lit., out from the hills)
- **akagetto** あかゲット plowboy

The term **akagetto** あかゲット is particularly interesting when you consider its literal meaning, "red blanket." At some time in Japan, red blankets must have been widely sold and used for warmth by the country people as they walked along the roads in winter. So much so that **akagetto** あかゲット became a synonym for a country oaf or hayseed.

Tsuchi-gumo 土蜘蛛 is defined as a contemptible country bumpkin. The literal meaning is "earth-spider," the word for a race of subhuman cave dwellers of early Japan.

Then there is **o-nobori-san** お上りさん, or 'honorable-climbing-person.' The honorifics **o** お and **san** さん are, of course, cynically meant, while **nobori** 上り suggests that the rural lout must rise from the uncultured depths whenever he is presumptuous enough to intrude in the rarified atmosphere of the capital.

Tagosaku 田吾作 also means clodhopper while **nōkyō-san** 農協さん is a more modern term deriving from the abbreviation for **Nōgyō Kyōdō Kumiai** 農業協同組合, or the "Federation of Agricultural Cooperative Associations." This federation arranged domestic and foreign tours for its members (mostly farmers), and the sight of these bright-eyed, camera-packing groups led by flag-carrying guides was a common one. Such tourists are meant by the term **nōkyō-san** 農協さん.

In Tokyo slang, we have the merciless construction **dasai-onna** ダサい女. The following exchange illustrates the expression's origin:

A: **Kichizaemon san no okusan ni aimashita ka. Hidoi wa yo.**
吉左衛門さんの奥さんに会いましたか。酷いわよ。
Did you meet Kichizaemon's wife? She's really awful.

B: **Naze?** 何故？ Why?

A: **Reigi-sahō wo shiranai otemba-san dakara yo.**
礼儀作法を知らないお転婆さんだからよ。
Because she's a boisterous minx who doesn't have any manners.

B: **Datte, Saitama desu mono.**
だって、埼玉ですもの。
But she's from Saitama (Prefecture), isn't she?

So to get **dasai-onna** ダサい女 we take the **da** だ of **datte** だって and the **sai** さい of Saitama 埼玉, thus, showing the contempt some of the fancy folk of Tokyo have for their country cousins from Saitama to the north.

The most scornful of all such expressions may well be **yamazaru** 山猿, or "mountain monkey"; the most common is the milder **inaka-mono** 田舎者, or "country person."

• **ki no kikanai inaka-mono** 気の利かない田舎者
  dull-witted hick

Sonna ki no kikan inaka-mono ni kiite mo muda da. そんな気の利かん田舎者に聞いても無駄だ。
It won't do any good to ask a dull clodhopper like that.

Two names often found among unlettered mental girls of low class are **Mī-chan** みいちゃん and **Hā-chan** はあちゃ

ん (**Mī-Hā** ミーハー). To call someone by these names indicates the low level of that person's tastes.

- **Mī-chan Hā-chan muki no eiga** みいちゃんはあちゃん向きの映画 a low-brow movie (lit., suited for **Mī-chan** みいちゃん, **Hā-chan** はあちゃん types)
- **Mī-chan Hā-chan muki no shōsetsu** みいちゃんはあちゃん向きの小説 a low-brow novel

The male equivalents of the above are **Hattsuan, Kuma-san** 八つぁん、熊さん (from **Hachikō, Kumakō** 八公、熊公) and are used in the same way.

Other expressions contemptuous of low-brows include:

- **doro-kusai onna** 泥臭い女 uncouth woman (**Doro-kusai** 泥臭い means smelling of mud.)
- **atsukamashii surekkarashi** 厚かましい擦れっ枯らし brazen hussy
- **nari-agari onna** 成り上がり女 upstart of a woman
- **zubutoi onna** 図太い女 cheeky woman

Ani wa nari-agari onna to kekkon shte chichi ni kandō sareta.
兄は成り上がり女と結婚して父に勘当された。
Because my elder brother married a worthless upstart of a woman, he was disowned by our father.

Hombun (One's Role in Society)
Persons of little accent can be traduced with virulent expressions like these:

- **gomi-tame yarō** ゴミ溜め野郎 scumbag
- **zako** 雑魚 pick-nose, small fry

Karera wa tada no zako ni suginai.
彼らはただの雑魚に過ぎない。
They're nothing more than small fry.

- **shōjin** 小人 Another word for small fry (lit.,
  small person)
- **Kono kusottare!** この糞ったれ！ You shitty little
  creep!
- **Kono iya na gaki-me.** この嫌な餓鬼め。 You odi-
  ous brat.
- **minohodo shirazu** 身の程知らず to not know
  one's place

**Tonari no hara-guroi babā wa minohodo shirazu
da.** 隣の腹黒い婆は身の程知らずだ That crafty old
woman next door does not know her place.

By now the reader may have noticed that **kono** この (this)
coupled with a noun of contempt, and **me** め (fellow, guy,
wretch) is one formula for a direct insult. **Me** め is the
Chinese character's **on** 音 reading and **yatsu** やつ is the **kun**
訓 reading. The spoken **yatsu** やつ is usually masculine, the
me め is quite as often feminine, as we have seen in other
examples. In any event, "You so-and-do!" is most readily
expressed by this formula: **Kono** この (so-and-so) **me**! め！

EMPLOYMENT
Censure is often achieved by referring to how people earn
their daily rice. In the entertainment field, we find:

- **diakon yakusha** 大根役者 poor actor (lit., giant
  radish actor)
- **joyū kuzure** 女優崩れ wreck of an actress, has-
  been actress
- **yakusha kuzure** 役者崩れ wreck of an actor

- **jari tarento** 砂利タレント television actor or actress who appears only a few times and then disappears from the scene for ever

(The likes of **jari-tarento** 砂利タレント infest Japanese television in such large numbers that I suspect that the oft-heard rumor is true—that the show producers promise to put these young hopefuls on television just to work their lusty wills on them, after which they give them the **hiji-deppō** 肘鉄砲, or "cold shoulder" (lit., elbow rifle). **Jari** 砂利 literally means gravel. **Ko-jari** 小砂利 (small gravel) is used to mean street urchins, and **tarento** タレント from the English "talent" has been adopted into Japanese to signify personality, as in a television personality, not special abilities.

Hearty maledicta can be heaped on writers in these three ways:

- **kakedashi no sammon bunshi**
  駆け出しの三文文士 amateur hack writer
- **heppoko bunshi** へっぽこ文士 penny-a-liner
- **ko‾shoku bungaku no kakedashi sakka**
  好色文学の駆け出し作家 fledgling writer of pornographic literature

Doubts are cast on the qualifications of men of medicine with the word **yaku-shiba** 藪医者, which means an ignorant doctor or quack:

Yabu-isha no kureta kusuri wo nondara obasan wa sugu ni nakunarimashita. 藪医者のくれた薬を飲んだら伯母さんはすぐに亡くなりました。
My aunt died immediately after taking the quack's medicine.

Ano otoko ga isha-datte? Tondemo nai hanashi da. Yabu-isha dokoro ka tada no seiyaku-gaisha no shain da zo.

あの男が医者だって？とんでもない話だ。藪医者どこ ろかただの製薬会社の社員だぞ。That man a doctor? That's absurd. He's not even a quack. He's just an employee of a pharmaceutical firm.

- **Hebo-isha** へぼ医者 also means quack. In fact **hebo** へぼ preceding any occupation raises doubts about qualifications:
- **hebo-bunshi** へぼ文士 writer of little skill
- **hebo-ekaki** or **hebo-gaka** へぼ絵描き／へぼ画家 dauber
- **hebo-shijin** へぼ詩人 poetaster
- **hebo-shokunin** へぼ職人 bungling workman
- **hebo-yakunin** へぼ役人 an incompetent official
- **yakunin no hashikkure** 役人の端っくれ a government official of low rank.

Are? Tada no yakunin no hashikkure da ze. Fuku-daijin no kaban-mochi da.

あれ？ただの役人の端っくれだぜ。副大臣の鞄持ちだ。 Him? He's just a low-ranking government official. He's not more than a briefcase carrier for the vice-minister.

Similar in meaning and usage to **hebo** へぼ (and **yabu** 藪) is **pē-pē** ペーペー, as in these examples:

- **pē-pē yakunin** ペーペー役人 a petty official
- **pē-pē yakusha** ペーペー役者 inferior actor
- **pē-pē zumō** ペーペー相撲 low ranking sumo wrestler

Sono pē-pē yakusha wa itsumo me-ue no hito ni peko-peko shite iru. そのペーペー役者はいつも目上の人にぺこぺこしている。
That inferior actor is always bowing and scraping to those above him.

Beginners at any gainful activity could be called **zubu no shirōto** ずぶの素人, or "rank amateurs."

At the bottom of the job-respect scale are:

Persons with no visible means of support, bums, vagrants or tramps, include:

- **fūraibō** 風来坊 tramp
- **furōsha** 浮浪者 vagrant
- **horōsha** 放浪者 bum
- **fūten** 瘋癲 a young vagrant, juvenile delinquent
- **furō no yakara** 浮浪の徒 street scum

Uchi no oi wa furōsha to shite omawari-san ni agerare-mashita. Hashi ni mo bō nimo kakaranai yatsu da. うちの甥は浮浪者としてお巡りさんに挙げられました。箸にも棒にも掛からない奴だ。
My nephew was picked up by a policeman for vagrancy. We haven't a prayer that he will ever be worth a fig.

Hashi ni mo bō ni mo kakaranai 箸にも棒にも掛からない literally means "can't even be snagged with [something as small and thin as] a chopstick or [as big and wide as] a stick."

CHAPTER SEVEN

Repugnant Personal Traits
(Ad Hominem Insults)

Most of us at one time or another are guilty of exhibiting undesirable behavior. Admitting to it, however, does not mean it can be forgiven or forgotten. In this chapter we will see with what impassioned invective the Japanese describe those deserving of such censure.

VANITY AND ARROGANCE

In a vertical society like Japan's, it is expected that people will play the game of butter up and trample down, with the tramplers taking on the colors of arrogance. What is puzzling to the Westerner, however, is that arrogance assumes the guise of paternalism and is widely accepted. On the other hand, vanity arising from appearance or possessions is frowned upon.

- **noboseagaru**　のぼせあがる　to be swollen with vanity

Jimbo-kun wa mada ketsu ga aoin da ga noboseagatte iru.
神保君はまだ尻が青いんだがのぼせあがっている。
Jimbo has little experience, but his head is swollen with vanity.

- **unuboreru**　自惚れる　to be vain; be conceited; have a high opinion of oneself

**Kare no okusan wa jibun de wa zessei no bijo da
to unuborete imasu.**

彼の奥さんは自分では絶世の美女だと自惚れていま
す。His wife fancies herself to be a peerless beauty.
(**Zessei no bijo**　絶世の美女　is a world-class beauty.)

SELFISH, COLD, AND CRUEL

The following behavior, although exhibited by most peo-
ples, is not so pronounced in Japan, where people display a
good amount of consideration (**omoiyari** 思いやり).

* **wagamama no gonge**　我儘の権化　living embodi-
  ment of selfishness
* **ingō jijī**　因業爺　cruel old man, scrooge
* **hana-tsumami-mono**　鼻摘まみ者　a heartless rat,
  a mean skunk (lit., a person or thing to hold one's
  nose at)

**Aitsu to kekkon shite wa ikan. Chi mo namida mo
nai hana-tsumami-mono da.**

あいつと結婚してはいかん。血も涙もない鼻摘まみ者
だ。Don't marry him. He's a heartless rat.

Chi mo namida mo nai　血も涙もない　means to have no
blood or tears.

* **reiketsu-kan**　冷血漢　cold-blooded villain

**Otōsan wa itsumo sonna koto iu wa. Mae no
iinazuke wa kangae no hinekureta reiketsu-kan
da to itta ja nai.**

お父さんはいつもそんなこと言うわ。前の許婚は考え
の捻くれた冷血漢だと言ったじゃない。
Dad, you always say something like that. You said
my last fiance was a cold-blooded villain with a
deranged mind.

- **wagamama no daimeishi** 我儘の代名詞 synonym for a selfish lout

Sono joyū no namae wa wagamama no daimeishi to narimashita.
その女優の名前は我儘の代名詞となりました。
The name of that actress has become synonymous with selfishness.

GRUMBLING
Complaining within the bosom of one's family was permitted in feudal Japan, but grumbling away from home especially in the presence of superiors was not to be tolerated.

- **Kono yakamashiya.** この喧し屋。 You grumbler.
- **guchippoi kijirushi** 愚痴っぽいキ印 bellyaching weirdo

GLUTTONY
Those who are slaves to their bellies are condemned with these words, all meaning glutton:

- **ō-gurai** 大喰らい
- **kuishimbō** 食いしん坊
- **taishokuka** or **bōshokuka** 大食家、暴食家

Kono taishokuka wa wagaya no tsura-yogoshi da. Uma hodo kuun da.
この大食家は我が家の面汚しだ。馬ほど食うんだ。
This glutton is a disgrace to our family. He eats like a horse.

MANNERS
Reigi 礼儀 and **reigi-sahō** 礼儀作法 are basic words for manners. **Reigi shirazu** 礼儀知らず means not to know one's manners. Other vocabulary in this context includes:

- **shitsuke ga warui kodomo** 躾が悪い子供 ill-mannered child
- **bushitsuke na yarō** 不躾な野郎 rude fellow
- **soya na kotoba-zukai** 粗野な言葉遣い rude language
- **yabo na otoko** 野暮な男 boorish man
- **futekusareta onna** 不貞腐れた女 sulky, ill-mannered wench
- **shitsurei** 失礼 impolite
- **burei** 無礼 rude
- **doro-kusai** 泥臭い uncouth (lit., stinking of mud)
- **no-sodachi** 野育ち born in a barn (lit., raised in a field)

Ima no hanashi no doro-kusai sonchō wa no-sodachi darō. 今の話の泥臭い村長は野育ちだろう。
The uncouth village chief we were talking about was probably born in a barn.

- **jakyō-to** 邪教徒 heathen
- **gōman burei** 傲慢無礼 haughty and rude

Mukashi sono kuni ni itte ita senkyōshi wa itsumo butsu-butsu itte imashita. Gōman burei na jakyō-to ni kakomarete iru kara fuyukai da to. 昔その国に行っていた宣教師はいつもぶつぶつ言っていました。傲慢無礼な邪教徒に囲まれているから不愉快だと。
The missionary who went to that country long ago was always complaining. He'd say how unpleasant it was to be surrounded by haughty and rude heathens.

- **ha ga uku** 歯が浮く to set one's teeth on edge, be repulsive (lit., one's teeth float)

Ano hito wa ha ga uku yō na koto wo iu otoko desu. あの人は歯が浮くようなことを言う男です。
That person is a man of repulsive and nauseating behavior (lit., he's enough to set one's teeth afloat).

STUBBORNNESS

Stubborn refusal to abide by the dictates of society and government in feudal Japan often brought harsh punishment to the recalcitrant.

- **ganko ittenbari** 頑固一点張り obstinacy itself

Shichō wa giron-gamashikute sono ue ganko ittenbari da.
市長は議論がましくてそのうえ頑固一点張りだ。The mayor is argumentative as well as extremely stubborn.

- **gō-tsukubari** 業突く張り a headstrong person; a diehard

Kono gō-tsukubari-me. この業突く張りめ。
You stubborn and unyielding fellow.

LIES, EXAGGERATION, AND SLANDER

Uso 嘘 is the most common word for "lie" and judging from the frequency with which it is heard, you would think that Japanese spend their days immersed in prevarication. This impression is aided by the multitudes of girls and young women whose every third word it seems is "**Uso!** 嘘！" which they employ much like the English "You don't say!"

- **mie-suita uso** 見えすいた嘘 obvious lie
- **shira-jirashii uso** 白々しい嘘 barefaced lie
- **hora-fuki no uso-tsuki** 法螺吹きの嘘つき boastful liar
- **gongo dōdan na uso-tsuki** 言語道断の嘘つき outrageous liar
- **hora** 法螺 big talk, hot air (**Hora** 法螺 is also the word for a trumpet shell.)
- **hora wo fuku** 法螺を吹く talk big, boast

- **hora-fuki** or **ōbora-fuki** 法螺吹き／大法螺吹き braggart, boaster; bull-shitter
- **hora-banashi** 法螺話 exaggerated story
- **dokuzetsu-ka** 毒舌家 person with a spiteful tongue
- **chūshō suru** 中傷する slander, fling dirt at a person's reputation

Kono shūkanshi ni wa Gō-san wa fuketsu na dokuzetsu-ka da to kaite arimasu. この週刊誌には郷さんは不潔な毒舌家だと書いてあります。
In this weekly magazine it is written that Mr. Go is a filthy man with a poison tongue.

Kanojo wa shiriai wo chūshō suru kuse ga aru.
彼女は知り合いを中傷する癖がある。
She has the habit of slandering all her acquaintances.

Gotō-san wa ōbora-fuki de hyōban desu.
後藤さんは大法螺吹きで評判です。 Mr. Goto has the reputation of being a well-known liar.

COWARDS AND SISSIES

Cowards are despised as much in Japan as elsewhere, but sissies, though looked down upon, do not receive as much opprobrium as in the West.

The first five words of the following fundamental vocabulary all mean coward:

- **okubyō-mono** 臆病者 coward
- **koshinuke** 腰抜け
- **hikyō-mono** 卑怯者
- **shōshin-mono** 小心者
- **funuke** 腑抜け
- **memeshii otoko** 女々しい男 sissy

- **yowamushi** 弱虫 wimp
- **niyaketa otoko** にやけた男 pantywaist
- **ikareponchi** いかれポンチ namby-pamby

The Japanese have at least two ways of making reference to a man who is bold and fearless (maybe even domineering) at home but mild-mannered and shy when facing the outside world, that is, a lion at home and a mouse abroad:

- **uchi-Benkei** or **kage-Benkei** 内弁慶／陰弁慶 a tiger at home (**Benkei** 弁慶 was a historical personage.)
- **ikuji-nashi** 意気地無し gutless sissy
- **chiisai ketsu no ana** 小さい尻の穴 cowardice (lit., small anus)

Kono ikuji-nashi no ketsu no ana wa donna ni chiisai deshō ka. この意気地無しの尻の穴はどんなに小さいでしょうか。
What a chicken-hearted coward this fellow must be (lit., I wonder how small this wimp's asshole is).

- **yowaimono-ijime** 弱い者苛め bully
- **okubyō** 臆病 cowardice

Sono yowaimono-ijime suru koshi-nuke no na wa okubyō no daimeishi to narimashita. その弱い者苛めする腰抜けの名は臆病の代名詞となりました。
That bully's name has come to stand for cowardice.

- **niyaketa** にやけた namby-pamby

Kono goro Tōkyō ni wa niyaketa gaijin no otoko ga ōi ne. この頃東京にはにやけた外人の男が多いね。
There are a lot of namby-pamby foreign men in Tokyo these days, aren't there?

WRONGDOING

It goes without saying that among a law-abiding people like the Japanese, those who violate laws are held in deep disdain indeed. And although even members of organized criminal gangs have a certain moral code of their own, they do not rate much higher in public esteem. Some basic words:

- **hannin** 犯人 criminal
- **zainin** 罪人 criminal
- **dorobō** 泥棒 thief
- **nusubito** or **nusutto** 盗人／盗っ人 thief
- **kosodoro** こそ泥 sneak thief
- **petenshi** ペテン師 con man
- **pakuri-ya** ぱくり屋 swindler
- **gorotsuki** ごろつき hooligan, hood
- **yota-mono** 与太者 a hooligan, rowdy

Aitsu wa keshikaran yota-mono da.
あいつは怪しからん与太者だ。
He is a damned hoodlum.

- **chō-honnin** 張本人 ringleader

Sono akumei-dakai chō-honnin wa mada tsuka-matte imasen.
その悪名高い張本人はまだ捕まっていません。
That infamouse ringleader still has not been caught.

- **jōshū-han** 常習犯 habitual criminal

Arabu sekai de wa mambiki no jōshū-han no te wo kiri-hanashimasu.
アラブ世界では万引きの常習犯の手を切り離します。
In the Arab world they cut off the hands of habitual shoplifters.

- **akudama**　悪玉　bad guy, villain (lit., a bad ball)

Seibugeki no akudama wa dōshite itsumo kuroi bōshiwo kabutte iru no kashira.　西部劇の悪玉はどうしていつも黒い帽子を被っているのかしら。
I wonder why the bad guys in Western movies always wear black hats.

Slang word that are equivalent to pilfer of filch are:

- **choromakasu**　ちょろまかす
- **kusuneru**　くすねる
- **kapparau**　かっぱらう

Sune ni kizu wo motsu 脛に傷を持つ literally means to have a scar on the shin, but figuratively means to have a shady past:

Zada-kun wa dō mo kusain da. Sune ni kizu wo motte irun ja nai ka.　座田君はどうも臭いんだ。脛に傷を持っているんじゃないか。
Zada really looks suspicious. I wonder if he doesn't have a shady past?

All sorts of crimes and criminals:

- **chijō ni yoru hanzai**　痴情による犯罪　a crime of blind passion

Furansu de wa chijō ni yoru hanzai no shobatsu wa wariai ni karui.
フランスでは痴情による犯罪の処罰は割合に軽い。
In France the punishment for a crime of passion is relatively light.

- **burai no shōnen** 無頼の少年 juvenile delinquents
- **machi no shirami** 街の虱 the criminal element
  (colloquial, lit., town lice)

**Sono burai no shōnen wa jiki ni machi no shirami
ni naru to omou.**
その無頼の少年はじきに街の虱になると思う。
I think those juvenile delinquents will eventually turn
into gangsters.

- **kusai meshi wo kuu** 臭い飯を食う
  to serve time in prison (lit., to eat smelly rice)

**Tsukamattara omae wa nagai aida kusai meshi
wo kuu koto ni naru darō.** 捕まったらお前は長い
間臭い飯を食うことになるだろう。
If you're caught, you'll be in prison for a long time.

- **babā-korogashi** 婆転がし swindling old women
- **jiji-korogashi** 爺転がし swindling old men

**Dōkyūsei no Wada wa babā-korogashi semmon
no sagi-shi da.**
同級生の和田は婆転がし専門の詐欺師だ。
My classmate Wada turned into a crook and special-
izes in swindling old women.

Inchiki いんちき is a handy and often-used word that means
false, fraudulent, phoney, or fake:

- **inchiki shōbai** いんちき商売 monkey business
- **inchiki-gusuri** いんちき薬 quack medicine
- **inchiki-gaisha** いんちき会社 bogus company
- **inchiki kabuya** いんちき株屋 fraudulent stock-
  broker

More crookedness:

- **ikasama** いかさま false, crooked

Mata nanika ikasama wo yaru no ka.
また何かいかさまをやるのか。
Are you going to do something crooked again?

LAZY, NO-GOOD SO-AND-SO'S

As industrious a race as the Japanese are, there are nonetheless those among them who pass their hours in idleness and contribute little to the betterment of themselves or others. They are described with the following:

- **nameke-mono** 怠け者 lazy fellow
- **norakura-mono** のらくら者 lazy fellow
- **guzu** 愚図 sluggard
- **yaku-tatazu** 役立たず good-for-nothing
- **goku-tsubushi** 穀潰し good-for-nothing
- **dame-otoko** ダメ男 no-good man
- **dema-onna** ダメ女 no-good woman
- **doku ni mo kusuri ni mo naran** 毒にも薬にもならん of no redeeming value (lit., can't become either medicine or poison)
- **roku-de-nashi** ろくでなし a good-for-nothing, a worthless fellow
- **kuso no yaku ni mo tatanai** 糞の役にも立たない worthless (lit., can't even be used for shit)

A: **Kon na roku-de-nashi wa kuso no yaku ni mo tachimasen. Kubi ni shitara ikaga deshō ka.**
こんなろくでなしは糞の役にも立ちません。首にしたらいかがでしょうか。
This rascal is not worth a shit. How would it be if I decapitated him?

B: **Kawaisō da to omowanai ka.**
可哀想だと思わないか。
Wouldn't you feel sorry for him?

A: **Zenzen. Datte doku ni mo kurusi ni mo naranai shiriomo ja nai desu ka.** 全然。だって
毒にも薬にもならない尻重じゃないですか。
Not in the least. Can't you see the loafer is of no value to anyone?

Shiri-omo 尻重 is a word for a loafer. It literally means "heavy ass." On those occasional mornings when I arise before my wife, it is my custom to call to her:

Oi! Shiri-omo-san! Okiro!
おい！尻重さん！起きろ！ Hey, loafer! Get up!

When, however, she is up before I am, she will soothe my sleep-befogged spirits with something like:

Kono sodai-gomi wa mada nete iru no. Hayaku oki-nasai. Koko wa yōrōin ja arimasen.
この粗大ゴミはまだ寝ているの。早く起きなさい。こ
こは養老院じゃありません。Is this slug-a-bed still asleep? Rise and shine. This is no old folks home.

Sodai-gomi 粗大ゴミ means oversized garbage. She's a sweetheart, my wife is. She won my heart the other day when she referred to me in passing as a **nure-ochiba** 濡れ落ち葉, "a wet leaf," in other words, a listless, lazy one.

TREACHERY, SHAMELESSNESS, HYPOCRISY, FLATTERY, AND INGRATITUDE
A cornucopia of unsavory traits of character:

- **on-shirazu** 恩知らず ungrateful wretch

Kono on-shirazu ni muchi no aji wo oshieyō.
この恩知らずに鞭の味を教えよう。
I'll give this ungrateful wretch a taste of the whip.

- **hara-guroi taiko-mochi**　腹黒い太鼓持ち　scheming toady (lit., a drum-carrier with a black stomach)

Sakki atta otoko wa itsumo chōjō ni peko-peko shite iru. Hara-guroi taiko-mochi da.
さっき会った男はいつも頂上にぺこぺこしている。腹黒い太鼓持ちだ。
The man we met earlier is always dancing attendance on his superiors. He is a scheming toady.

- **haji-shirazu**　恥知らず　shameless

Sono haji-shirazu no on-kise-gamashii taido wa keshikaran.
その恥知らずの恩着せがましい態度は怪しからん。
The condescending attitude of that shameless fellow is damnable.

- **osekkai na gomasuri**　お節介なゴマすり　meddlesome toadies

Daitōryō no mawari ni o-sekkai na gomasuri ga ōzei atsumatte imasu.　大統領の周りにお節介なゴマすりが大勢集まっています。Many meddlesome toadies are gathered around the president.

- **uragiri-mono**　裏切り者　traitor
- **gizensha**　偽善者　hypocrite
- **neko-kaburi**　猫被り　hypocrisy
- **tsura-yogoshi**　面汚し　disgrace (lit., a face-black-ener)

- **futa-gokoro** 二心 treacherous flatter (lit., two hearts)
- **chōchin-mochi** 提灯持ち a flatterer (lit., a lantern bearer, the person who went at the head of a group to light the path for the others)

Shōtai wo kotowatta yo. Ano yō na futa-gokoro ga aru chōchin-mochi no apāto ni iku mon ka.
招待を断ったよ。あのような二心がある提灯持ちのア パートに行くもんか。I refused the invitation. Under no circumstances would I enter the apartment of that treacherous flatterer.

RASCALITY IN GENERAL
If you cannot find the zinger you are searching for among all the preceding, proceed just a little ways further.

- **shōne no kusatte iru** 性根の腐っている depraved (lit., spiritually rotten)

Sono shōne no kusatte iru nariagari-mono wa mainichi tsura-ate wo iun desu.
その性根の腐っている成り上がり者は毎日面当てを言 うんです。That depraved upstart says something spiteful every day.

- **darashi no nai** だらしのない slovenly

Naze sono darashi no nai abazure wo yatottan da.
何故そのだらしのないあばずれを雇ったんだ。
Why did you hire that slovenly wench?

- **egetsu-nai** えげつない vulgar
- **egetsu-nai gokuaku-nin** えげつない極悪人 vulgar villain of the worst sort
- **yakubyō-gami** 疫病神 a jinx

Aitsu wa yakubyō-gami da. Issho ni nottara kotchi no kuruma wa kitto jiko wo okosu.
あいつは疫病神だ。一緒に乗ったらこっちの車はきっと事故を起こす。He (she) is a jinx. If he (she) rides in our car, we'll surely have wreck.

- **hinekureta seikaku no hito**　捻くれた性格の人
  someone with a warped mind
- **kawari-mono**　変わり者　a crank
- **ijiwaru babā**　意地悪婆　cantankerous old woman

I hope this book has enabled you to recognize the many forms of direct defamation and has provided you, if attacked, with the weapons to lay about with insulting abuse and hearty curses.